PERMISSION GRANTED

DISCOVER HOW LIFE
CHANGES

PERMISSION
GRANTED

PERMISSION TO GRIEVE

First Edition

Copyright © 2020 Kate Butler Books

www.katebutlerbooks.com

All rights reserved.

ISBN: 979-8-9883184-1-5

Design by Margaret Cogswell
margaretcogswell.com

With love, we dedicate this book to Linda Mitchell, Patty's mother, who originally gave her permission to show up and be seen. We also dedicate this book to the women of previous generations who had far greater constraints than permission. We stand on the shoulders of those women, and in order to properly honor them, we must now grant ourselves permission to stand up, show up, and be seen.

We especially want to mention some of our mentors and friends who have supported us in so many ways along the way. Thank you, Janet Attwood, for supporting this project from the get-go. Thank you, Lisa Nichols, for reminding us that when we give ourselves permission to show up for ourselves, anything is possible. To Marci Shimoff, for helping us along the way, and for offering support over the last 30 years. To Iyanla Vanzant, who taught us that God gave us permission to be seen when we were born. Thank you from the bottom of our hearts.

And last but not least, to women everywhere,
YOU are the reason we wrote this book.
Collectively we can and will make a difference.

WE SINCERELY HOPE THIS BOOK INSPIRES
YOU TO LIVE YOUR LIFE TO THE FULLEST.

TABLE OF CONTENTS

TABLE OF CONTENTS

*I don't need anybody's
permission to be
remembered.*

*I will be. Whether
they like it or not.*

LADY GAGA

YOU ARE PRE-APPROVED

IYANLA VANZANT

As someone who grew up half African American, half Native American, I give a whole new meaning to mixed race.

I think for me, growing up I didn't have a role model. I didn't have a model of success. I didn't have an acceptable model of womanhood. I mean, my grandmother was a Native American housekeeper, and my mom was an African American alcoholic.

I grew up in the 1950s when, if your skin color wasn't right, there was no one to look up to and admire. Now however, in the 21st Century, who we are as women is shifting and changing. And it's changing so much that it's up to us to create new icons—amazing women who our granddaughters and great-granddaughters will see as legends worth admiring and mirroring.

I know this book is about giving yourself permission, so I wanted to just tell you a little story. Whenever I speak at events, I never write down what I'm going to say. It's pretty scary to most people, but I've learned over these 28 years to just listen and let Spirit guide me. One day, I was scheduled to speak at a huge church in Los Angeles, Agape Spiritual Center. I was going to speak there, but I had no message.

I prayed and meditated about it, but . . . no message. On the way out of my house, I grabbed my mail from the mailbox. *Let me go through it in the car*, I said to myself. And, as I was going through the mail, I saw an envelope with a headline that read, *You Are Pre-Approved!*

"Thank you, God," I said aloud. "That's my message."

I actually preached an entire 35-minute sermon from that single envelope I got in the mail. And isn't that such an important message for us as women?

You are pre-approved.

We all came to this Earth pre-approved. You came here approved with all your pieces and parts in place and—even the parts that fall down—you've got the equipment to pick them back up. Your mind, for instance, is your most powerful tool; it can create or destroy based on your choices. Your mouth is a womb. You give birth every day with your womb, and your words—which are conceived when your mind and your heart are in alignment—represent that. We as women have to get out of this consciousness, this thinking, that somebody has to approve us.

Approval is an inside job and, too often, we look outside of ourselves for the approval that *we can give ourselves.*

We rely on somebody else to say we're okay. I cannot tell you what it was like for me as a woman of color, first of all, to be a life coach. God bless Thomas Leonard who put me in his experimental group. Yes, I was an experiment before Thomas created the global coach-training movement: Coach U. There was me and Karen MacDonald—the only two women of color, the only two people of color in the group when Thomas was about to start Coach U.

I've been an experiment. And I was okay with it.

As a woman of color, as a coach, as a Metaphysical Minister in a world that's inundated with traditional religious and faith concepts, I am a freak of nature. The thing I learned early on is that I couldn't ask people for approval. I had to ask them for support. If they didn't support me, then I would just move on to the next person.

We are pre-approved as women. We have to stop trying to get other people's approval and learn how to get their support by asking for what we need and being willing to move on to the next person if we get a "no."

You are pre-approved for the divine ideas that you're birthing in this new age—including the idea that, as women, we are going to do things, create things and bring forward things that nobody has ever seen before.

You are pre-approved; you have ideas that nobody is going to be able to tell you how to do because they haven't been done before— or it hasn't been done the way we, as a woman, would do it.

I learned a long time ago that the only one I needed approval from was me.

I had to be clear about who I am as a woman . . . who I am as a teacher and healer. I had to stop asking people to approve me because I am pre-approved. I came here that way, and I was put on this planet to be exactly who I am.

Where you are and what you're thinking, what you're feeling, and what's being birthed in your mind, speak life to that and know that you have the approval of the Universe. You have the approval of the goddess of life . . . the approval of your Source, your Creator, and Mother Earth to create *simply because you're a woman!*

You don't need approval for that. You came here like that. Use this power to the best of your ability and don't be so willing to give up what comes through you—what's being birthed through you— simply because nobody's ever done it before you. Whatever it is, it's for *you* to do. You are pre-approved to do it. Your permission has already been granted!

Go forth and live your purpose. The world is waiting.

INTRODUCTION

PATTY AUBERY

Goodbye, I sobbed as my mother's hand slowly went limp in mine. It was July 3, 2012, and the strong-willed defender and ever-present supporter of my remarkable life was gone.

It had been a good journey, the two of us. Through life's ups and downs . . . across a career that spanned from unexciting to extraordinary . . . and now into an uncertain future without her, my mom had been with me and my family every step of the way.

By that point in my life, I'd been the President and chief rainmaker behind one of the most successful publishing brands in history: *Chicken Soup for the Soul*. Its two founding coauthors—Jack Canfield and Mark Victor Hansen—were famous and rich beyond belief. But few people outside of the company really knew the sheer force of will and determination it had taken to build that empire—

or about the role I had played during countless nights of working late, weeks of stress bringing hundreds of book titles to print on time, and managing licensing deals that ran the gamut from television to recorded music to greeting cards, pet food, calendars, educational products and more. I was also Jack Canfield's Chief Executive Officer, his greatest champion, and the guardian of his career.

But all that was about to change.

"Promise me," my mom begged on our last day together, "promise me you won't hide behind that man. I didn't raise a daughter to be invisible. Promise me you will show up and be seen."

I promised my mom that day. I could no longer hide. It was time to give myself permission to be seen.

Permission granted has been my mantra ever since.

* * * *

What does it take to build a billion-dollar brand for someone else? What kind of woman would spend 18 years of her life creating a legacy for someone else to leave behind? During the heyday of *Chicken Soup*, I not only oversaw the production and publication of 230 different *Chicken Soup* titles, I also co-authored 14 of the books myself. I remember the week we had seven different books on the *New York Times* bestseller list at the same time. It was a Guinness World Record, and yet I still felt it was all luck. If hard work had a hand in it—or in any of the other monumental achievements we enjoyed in those days—I gave the credit to my business partners, Jack and Mark.

When the time came to promote the 14 different *Chicken Soup for the Soul* titles that I had coauthored with the two of them, I traveled the country doing book signings and television appearances—once when I was pregnant with my second child. One of my books, *Chicken Soup for the Christian Soul,* rolled out with the largest first printing ever for a nonfiction title. Yet I never gave myself permission to OWN my success. I was waiting for someone to acknowledge me . . . to tell me I had arrived . . . to put me up on some pedestal that didn't even exist.

I waited a long time. Until, one day, I didn't wait anymore. We've all heard the saying, *If it's meant to be, it's up to me.* So, relying solely on the same determination and force of will I'd employed for years, I began a journey to the different life I knew was my calling.

I gave myself permission to combine the personal-growth and human-potential knowledge I'd studied, lived and produced for years and bring it to the women's market as a champion for others who needed to step into their own limelight.

My first assignment, a women's retreat in Santa Barbara where a dozen professionals, entrepreneurs and authors gathered, was the ideal format for me to teach what I knew.

It was filled to capacity with women who wanted to learn from me. And I was scared to death.

Reaching out to my friend, Teresa Huggins, I asked if she would co-facilitate the weekend training with me. Candidly, I had no idea how to run a retreat alone, and I certainly didn't have the confidence. But I had made a promise, and the promise needed to be kept.

As the women eagerly assembled at our luxury location that first day of the retreat, I reflected that it was almost a year to the day after my mom had passed away. I'll never forget the fear of stepping out on my own in an industry that had been dominated by men I both knew and worked with—and I probably said 20 words that whole weekend as Teresa guided the women in their studies. But together we did it.

I did it, and I survived.

What I realized during that scary, beautiful weekend was that everything leading up to that point was all perfect. The only one who could have given me *permission to be me*, was me. In order to fully step into my power, I had to become my complete self. When I showed up fully—as I did that weekend—I realized that I was also giving other women permission to do the same.

It was so simple, yet it still felt so difficult. But still I leaned into this new version of myself and began a beautiful journey. The awesome part of it was that I had really lived it: I was doing what needed to be done, I just wasn't owning the results.

I also realized that, early in my career, I was so busy being busy that I didn't take the time to celebrate my success. Additionally, I'd felt guilty about trying to be a mom and an executive at the same time. Within a year after my husband Jeff and I were married, the first *Chicken Soup* book started to take off. It had taken five long years and 16-hour days to bring this labor of love to fruition, to find a publisher who would take a risk on us, and to market the book to bestseller status. Within weeks of the book starting to take off, I discovered that I was pregnant with my first son. What was I to do? Should I quit my amazing job and raise a family, or struggle onward as a working mom?

I wanted both. I knew I could do it. But was I being selfish?

I knew in my bones that being at the helm of *Chicken Soup for the Soul* was a once-in-a-lifetime career opportunity, but with that knowledge came tremendous guilt, too: not being there for every mealtime, saying goodnight over the phone from a hotel room thousands of miles away, and missing the little celebrations like a smiley face returned on a crumpled page of homework.

What I didn't know at the time was that being immersed in building that brand—building something celebrated and lasting—was one of the greatest gifts I could have given to my boys. I became an accidental role model. I showed them what it looked like to live one's passion and life purpose—and that, when you do live authentically, everything else falls into place. Happiness, health and wealth are actually byproducts of pursuing something you are passionate about!

What a concept.

I just wish that I had had a woman mentor back in those days to stand beside me and tell me it would all be okay. If only a female role model had been there before me and could have shown me the way.

Instead, I navigated those waters alone. And there were many days I truly felt alone. When I was at work, I felt I should be at home. When I was at home, I felt as though I should be at work. The guilt was ever-present, nearly driving me crazy.

I remember the defining moment of my struggle: as I sat in my publisher's private jet, flying to a book signing, I was riddled with guilt that I should be at home with my husband and boys. Here I was on a private plane, living my dream—yet I was miserable. So miserable in fact, that I knew I needed to make a decision. I had to give myself permission to be present and enjoy that moment. I had to let go of all the other stories in my head. I decided—then and there—that, when I was home, regardless of the time we had together, I would be present with my family. When I was at work, I would do the same.

I suddenly realized that—in order to assuage my guilt—I'd actually been looking to others for approval. I waited for approval from my husband, my neighbors, my business partners, anyone who would say, *Patty, you're doing the right thing.*

The reality was that *approval* was something I needed to find on the inside. I needed to grant myself permission. And so, over the years, this mental battle remained a constant theme in my life. I would get the message—give myself approval—just until the next obstacle or limiting belief showed up, causing me to think, *Didn't I learn this already?*

But what were those obstacles, really? They were actually opportunities which would take me to the next level of success. They were stairsteps on my journey. And each level brought me more awareness about my own desires, as well as more conviction that I had the ability to choose.

They were also lessons that allowed me to be more compassionate towards myself and, in turn, be more compassionate toward others.

* * * *

What did I ultimately learn that I can now pass on to other women? At the end of the day, no one goes it alone. Success really is a team sport and it does take a village. What I needed more than anything back in those days was a cheerleading squad not only to cheer me on, but to say, *You can do it. We believe in you.* As a woman, I was a tremendous cheerleader for my husband, my kids and my business partners. But when it came to me, I couldn't summon up the same enthusiasm. I had to eventually find it for myself.

And I did.

I reached out to other women I admired like Janet Attwood who wrote *The Passion Test*, and Lisa Nichols from the movie, *The Secret*. They could see in me what I couldn't see in myself. And when I shared my hopes and dreams with them, they were there to hold me accountable and cheer me on. They were there to make sure I showed up no matter what—letting nothing get in the way. It was a huge thing to have that support. It was so powerful.

I decided as a result of these supportive relationships that I would pay it forward. For the first time in my life, I knew for certain that I was living my life purpose. I vowed to help others live their life purpose, too. I pledged to motivate and support other women to live the life of their dreams—giving them permission to never settle, never play small, and take credit where credit is due.

It's the kind of permission I never received from anyone until I granted permission to myself.

Today, my boys are grown and in their 20's. My husband and I have survived 27 years of marriage, and our nanny is still part of the family. When I think back, I wonder: if I had settled and kept playing small . . . if I had not asked myself the question, *What more is there for me if I simply step up?* . . . if I didn't pursue the dream that I could have it all, what kind of life would I have had? It's safe to say that my life, then and now, would be drastically different. I wouldn't have worked with thousands of women around the world. I wouldn't have made amazing, lifelong friendships with so many people I've met through the work I do. And I wouldn't have the war stories and experiences behind me to remind me that I've done scary things before, and I can do them again.

What drives me today is helping to bring about a world where every woman digs deep within her soul and asks herself the big question: *what do I want for ME?* Not to please someone else, but to allow her to live her dream and be the person she was meant to be. To understand that this lifetime is not a competition, but a collaboration—a chance to create community and support. To recognize that each of us needs to go the extra mile and believe that we can.

If I can overcome my limiting beliefs and grant myself permission, anyone can. Together we are better—and together we can *and will* make a difference.

PATTY AUBERY

Patty is the President of The Canfield Training Group, Patty Aubery has not only overseen the growth of the publishing industry's first billion-dollar brand, as the President of Chicken Soup for the Soul®, but she's also created a multi-million dollar training company around the success principles of author Jack Canfield. Patty has expanded these live training and coaching programs to 108 countries and prepared thousands of emerging success trainers for professional careers in the transformational field. She is a #1 NY Times bestseller.

She is the CVO for GoalFriends, and she is now dedicated to bringing her experience to women entrepreneurs, sales professionals, and corporate employees through live events, retreats, women's summits and speaking engagements that teach audiences and small groups the Success Principles and strategic career planning. You can reach Patty at www.pattyaubery.com

"Give yourself permission to tell the truth to yourself."

IYANLA VANZANT

PERMISSION TO
RECEIVE MIRACLES

KATE BUTLER

*S*ince ancient times Europeans believed that number 7 represented the unity of God and universe. It is said that Angel number 7 is related to inner wisdom, mysticism, intuition and inner strength. If you see this number, it means that you should have more faith in your guardian angels, but also in your own abilities.

I was born on 7/7.

When I am driving, I feel like I am free. The moment I got my driver's license felt like the opening of a new world for me. Long distance drives and road trips were at the very top of my favorite things to do. In fact, as an East Coast girl, growing up I always dreamed of living in sunny California. As I got older, my dreams became reality. I had the adventure of a lifetime as I packed up my little Nissan Sentra with everything I could possibly fit and drove from Southern New Jersey all the way across the country until I reached that Pacific Coast Highway. The drive itself was as much a dream come true as it was for me to rent my first studio apartment in Newport Beach, CA.

I have always been one to follow my heart. I have been known to go after dreams both big and small. I have been known to take big chances and even bigger risks if it meant a shot at living out the wild ideas that would swirl in my imagination. The move to California at 23-years-old was risky and dreamy, all wrapped into one journey.

Fate brought me to California, where I met my husband, Mel. Looking back, I know this was one of the biggest reasons my heart was pulling me there. And as fate would have it, we were both from the East Coast. So, when we decided to settle down, we made the choice to move back east and begin our life together. We got married, bought a home, started a family, and created a beautifully busy and rewarding life. Like any family, we experience our ups and downs. I choose to cling tighter to the ups, so I remember these events more clearly. However, there are other moments that are etched in my memory forever and one of those experiences happened one fateful October day.

On a cool, crisp October morning on the East Coast, all things were apropos at a glance…but if you took a closer look, you would have seen a much different story. On that morning, I was once again looking forward to a long road trip. I was going from my home in New Jersey to a business conference in Washington, D.C.

As a professional success coach, I flew all around the country attending seminars to learn and connect into the community. Now, I'm not crazy about flying. So, I was so pleased this conference was local, and I could drive there in my own car. This was a great networking opportunity and it was only a few hours away. It seemed like a huge win-win, so it felt strange that whenever I tried to buy my ticket to the event, the site wouldn't let me finish the purchase.

My daughters, Bella and Livie, were very small at the time. I would put them to bed at night and have my work time for as long as I had the brain power. I spent a good three or four nights trying to buy these tickets. On the fourth night, I got a call from the registration team saying, "We see you're in the checkout, but you haven't registered yet."

They thought I didn't want to buy the ticket. I said, "No. You don't understand. I'm trying to buy the ticket. It's not allowing me to purchase it." They ended up giving me a free upgrade and it sounded like a great deal. I thought alright, this a good sign. And I decided, "I'm going."

That was seven weeks before the conference; and in the days that followed, I kept getting these intuitive messages that I wasn't supposed to go. Sometimes it was a feeling in the pit of my stomach, and other times the image of the conference would come into my awareness during meditation and leave me feeling apprehensive and nervous. They were starting to bother me. I remember sitting in my family room with my best friend Felicia while our children played together. I said, "Felicia, I am not supposed to go to this event."

She said, "What do you mean?"

I told her, "I'm getting the weirdest feelings and intuitive hits. I have these visions that I'm not supposed to go. I've started to think about it multiple times a day. I just have this really icky feeling that something is off."

She said, "Well, that's really unlike you because you normally get super excited to attend these events." She continued, "I'll watch the kids. Why don't you go discuss it with Mel? If you really feel that strongly about it—Just don't go."

I went into the kitchen and called my husband at work. I never call him at work. He is usually working in a classified area, and he's not allowed to have his phone in the room. I expected to leave him a message, but he answered.

Now, you have to know my husband to get the humor of this next part. Mel is not one to waste good money. When I explained what was going on, he said, "Well, did you already pay for the ticket?"

He put his half-joking aside and did his best to support me.

"I think you're just nervous about leaving the kids again. You've been travelling a lot." He said, "I've got them. You don't have to get on a plane. You'll be gone a day and a half. It's an easy trip."

Then, he assured me, "They will be fine."

I said, "You're right." I tucked it all away.

That was on a Tuesday. Friday morning, I was ready to leave for the event. The babysitter was at the house and with the kids. My suitcase was packed. I had on a cute black sundress. My whole look was put together.

I stopped to put on deodorant, and I dropped it. It rolled down the front of my black dress leaving a huge white streak. I'd never done that before; I've never done it since. And I thought, "Wow, this is super interesting and then I thought, here we go again."

I scrubbed my dress until it came clean, but I just couldn't get on the road. I came back in the house six more times. I forgot my sunglasses, my cell phone, my charger, my business cards, my comfy shoes, and to leave the babysitter my husband's phone number.

Seven times I went back into the house, causing me to leave almost an hour later than I had planned.

Finally, I was sitting in the car, I looked down and the necklace I was wearing was broken in half. *Really!* I thought. I just took the necklace off. *I'm not going back in. If I am going, then I just have to go.* I put on Brené Brown's audio book, whatever it was at the time, and I pressed play.

Now, part of the reason I love a good road trip is because I get uninterrupted time with a great audiobook—which I adore. So, when I tell you that the next thing I know it was an hour and 15 minutes into the drive, and I hadn't heard one thing this woman had said, this was not only highly unusual, it was on the verge of disturbing. I mean, I could not tell you one single thing from that book. I was on I-95 South, and I could not remember how I got there. The last thing I remembered was putting the broken necklace on the seat next to me and starting the audio book.

The next exit was Bel Air, Maryland. I was familiar with the exit because I'd hosted retreats for some of my clients in that town. I also knew there was a Chick-fil-a nearby. I decided to pull off and get an iced tea, hoping the caffeine would wake me up.

The next part of this journey I remember as if it were yesterday. The Chick-fil-a was in a shopping center that was a good mile and a half down the road from the exit. As soon as I pulled in, I saw them. The signs. They were everywhere.

I can't say what order the signs were in, but they said "Caution," "Warning," "Stop," "Do Not Enter." There were seven signs all with the same basic message, "Do Not Proceed." No construction was going on. It wasn't normal. And I said, "Oh my God, these signs are for me."

I was already in the drive through lane. I put my car in park.

* * *

A few months before this, I'd attended a retreat at Kripalu in the Berkshires. During my time there, I learned about angels in a different way than ever before. The theory was that angels worship us because we can experience things in physical form, where they are all energetic form, and usually it's perceived to be the other way around where we believe they have all the magic and power. However, we have this power of choice and human experience, and it's up to us to invite our angels into our experience.

The angels are around us all the time. In a very few circumstances, they'll step in without being invited. However, you can call your angels in at any time. As soon as you do, they are waiting to come in and help.

I found the theory so interesting. I'd started using it every time I would travel, which was mainly on planes. Since flying isn't my favorite pastime, this new ritual made such a significant difference in my experience. I would feel more relaxed, more peaceful, and most importantly, I felt completely protected. So, before every flight, I would call in my angels to guard and protect the plane.

* * *

As soon as I saw those signs in the parking lot, I knew this was a moment I needed protection, and I knew intuitively that it was critical that I call my angels in. It was a strange feeling, actually it was polarizing. One part of me was saying this can't be real, everything is fine and the other, much louder part of me was saying, although I'm not sure what I need protection from, I am feeling a sense of urgency that I need support and protection. I need a miracle in this moment. So, I said, "Angels, please come in. Please surround me, support me, and protect me. I don't know what protection I need; but I know I need you. I know I need protection now." I imagined my primary or guardian angels surrounding all four corners of my car and then I imagined another layer of angels all around.

As soon as I did this, it hit me. I realized I'd had signs for months—the ticket I couldn't buy, the visions, the intuitive feeling in the pit of my stomach each time I would think about the event, the dress, the necklace, the sunglasses—and now actual literal signs right in front of me telling me to stop, to not proceed, to have caution.

I opened my eyes, took my car out of park, ordered my iced tea, and drove around to pick it up.

I got back on I-95 South. Not ten minutes after getting back on the highway, I was hit.

A man slammed his car into mine at 80 miles an hour. In the split second before impact, I saw him and turned my wheel to go onto the shoulder. I thanked God I was the left-hand lane—my first miracle.

There was construction up ahead, and the shoulder wouldn't last much longer. It would be a blessing if our cars stopped before hitting the cement barriers, and they did. This would be my second miracle.

He was pushing us both along the guardrail, sliding and scraping. I looked over and realized we were elevated. I could see the northbound lanes of I-95 running below me. If we flipped over the guardrail, we would land on the busy interstate and it would be over. I prayed for another blessing that my car would not flip. This would be my third miracle.

And, the car seats. I looked at the empty car seats in my rear-view mirror as I was crashing. So, how long could this have been? Three seconds. Yet, all of this was going really fast in my mind.

I thought, *Thank God they're not here!* My fourth miracle.

The moment was so much bigger. I felt this fierce resistance—there was just no way I was leaving them. And I was not leaving. I had a life mission. Miracle five.

I remember saying, "I refuse to leave my family. I refuse to leave my life purpose. I have so much more to do. No! I will fight in this moment. I will fight to stay. I will NOT go."

And then everything stopped. Miracle number six.

Every single airbag had gone off, everything was crashed in, glass was everywhere. I didn't call 9-1-1; I called my husband. Then, I lost it. Then, I was hysterical.

The police arrived and they couldn't believe I was walking out of the car on my own. My car was destroyed, yet I had not one broken bone. This was miracle number seven.

The man who hit me received seven citations at the scene of the accident. People have asked me, "Did you sue him?" The answer is, "No. He was my angel. I prayed for guidance and protection and within ten minutes it was given to me. I was not supposed to get to my destination. The crash saved me from what I was going to experience over the weekend; something I was not supposed to encounter. After the accident, I received clear and vivid visions of what I would have encountered if I had made it to my destination.

I was clear this man was one of my angels.

Prior to this, when I would have these premonitions or miracles occur I would second guess by asking "is this real" or "is it really as powerful as I think it is" or "did that really just happen?" And I would play tricks with myself. I would start to gather evidence on how it "made more sense" another way. Or, I would convince myself I could not have just "known that," I must have read or seen it somewhere that I just don't recall.

We play these games with ourselves. We look for ways to disprove the miracle.

All of us have superpowers. We can dismiss or discount our gifts because they come so naturally to us that we sometimes think *they can't be that powerful,* and yet they are. Our gifts are actually the most powerful things we have.

This experience allowed me to recognize just how strong my intuition is and how deeply it can and should be trusted. I have now given myself permission to -trust my intuition, even when it doesn't add up or make sense. I have given myself permission to trust the intuitive messages I receive daily through meditation, and I allow myself to be guided by a higher power believing the universe is always conspiring in my favor, even if I cannot see it at the time.

This experience gave me permission to trust my intuitive abilities, but it also gave me a strong sense of purpose to share my abilities with the world and help others do the same. When I was faced with that exit point and made that very conscious decision that I "would not go" and that I "had to stay," something powerful awoke inside of me that was bigger than me.

This was when I began connecting to my clients and audience in a whole new way. Once I gave myself permission to fully stand in my gifts, it was as if something had been lifted for those around me as well. I had client after client begin to approach me about sharing their gifts and purposes with the world.

This eventually turned into what is now known as the Inspired Impact Book Series. It began with 20 women sharing their powerful stories to bring their gifts to the world in a bigger way. The success of that first book led to the second, and we are now on our seventh book in the series. We have more than 200 authors who are part of our #1 International Best-selling series.

There are so many ways my gifts have showed up since the crash. As an Intuitive Success Coach, Strategist and Publisher, I am now able to fully show up for myself and my clients. I recently published a children's book, and during the author's best-seller celebration she interviewed me and asked, "How did you come up with the calendar scene and your vision for the ending? Those two things tied the whole book together!"

I said, "I hope your audience doesn't mind if I get a bit spiritual. My job is to be the conduit for your art to be expressed in the world. I have the honor of holding the space, and my job is to connect with our higher power, tap into your unique vision and gifts and then receive. I am able to receive divine downloads that do not come from me but come from infinite intelligence and are sent for the highest and best of all involved. When we are able to pause, reflect and open ourselves up to receive these downloads, what comes through is given to us to make the world a better place. My job is just to translate that to you."

To simply say "lesson learned" would be a bit too easy.

I continued to get "tested" to see if I *really* learned the lesson.

Most recently, I was scheduled to attend one of my mentor's events in California. As I began to schedule the trip, the flight times weren't aligning, and I was getting a ticket through a friend to help out another friend—the whole thing felt sort of makeshift. I remember thinking, I've attended this same event for the past six years, and it's always just been easy, but this time it wasn't. How interesting…

I was planning on going, but it turned out that none of the flights were working out. The timing was wrong. I was facing flying out of all these different airports. I thought, this is so weird.

I meditated on it which is what I'll do now when I want to check in to be clear. I mean, sometimes the flights just don't work; and you check the next day, and they do. So, this is how I've learned my lesson. I don't guess if it's a message. I meditate to truly explore and take the time and see what is truly showing up for me.

I dialed in on the trip and got this crazy message. This was in January of 2020. The message I got was something unsettling was about to happen. Not that something bad would happen at the event; not that something bad would happen to me; but that I was not supposed to go to this event, or anywhere for that matter. I clearly got this message.

I began cancelling all of the trips I had scheduled. One trip in particular affected many people. It was a big event that many of us had planned for months. I had clients who were looking forward to meeting me, and now I was having to explain why I wasn't coming. I disappointed a lot of people, and all I could say was, "I don't know how else to explain this, other than to tell you, I cannot go. I'm not supposed to be there. I don't think anything bad is going to happen at the event, but for some reason, I'm not supposed to go. Something is happening, and I have to stay where I am."

Three weeks later, everyone was reaching out to me because the coronavirus, COVID-19, had arrived in the United States, and it was spreading. Travel bans were enforced. People were told to stay home. Our country began to shelter in place. Everyone wanted to know, was this what you were talking about? Yes, it was. I didn't know exactly how it would transpire, but this was absolutely what I was seeing and feeling during my meditations.

This was a huge lesson for me on trusting. I had no idea what would show up, or how it would show up, but I received intuitive guidance that I needed to remain home with my family. I needed to trust that. And I did.

When we have a vision or dream, we cannot see the whole thing and do not know how it will play out, but if we trust the intuitive guidance along the way, it will unfold. It most likely will not look the way we thought, but in my experience, it is always better than we ever could have imagined.

I now also ask myself where there could be angels in disguise, and I look for miracles daily. Most people would not consider a man who hit your car at 80 miles per hour to be an angel, but I know he was. There are many angels in our life, and we begin to consider how the divine is always setting us up for the next best thing, we can begin to ask, who may be an angel in disguise?

One of the mantras I say each day is "I am open to the infinite miracles that are available to me today." And it is very rare a day will go by without me recognizing a miracle. These miracles show up in a phone call from a friend I had been missing and wanting to hear from. They show up in travels when I never, and I mean never, hit traffic; and when I am late, I always, and I mean always, catch my flight. Miracles show up in protection when my kids take a nasty spill off their bike that should have been a million times worse, but somehow, they are fine. They show up when severe thunderstorms surrounded our area and could have been devastating for the construction of our pool, but somehow missed only our house just as workers were finishing up the final touches. Miracles come in receiving that huge endorsement for a book cover, just in the nick of time, moments before the book goes to publish. And they also come disguised sometimes, but if you look closer, and if you choose to see them, miracles are everywhere, both big and small.

Most people would consider these things to be coincidences and discount them as such. I know they are miracles. If you discount them, why would they bother to return to you? By honoring them, you open yourself to receive miracles day after day.

I now give myself permission to honor the process, trust the signs and trust myself. It may not make sense at first, but if my experiences have taught me anything, it's that when you trust your inner knowing, your outer world will be supported by infinite miracles.

KATE BUTLER, CPSC

Kate Butler is a #1 International best-selling and Award-winning author and speaker. As a CPSC, Certified Professional Success Coach, she offers clients dynamic programs to help them reach their ultimate potential and live out their dreams. She does this through Mindset, Success and Book Publishing programs. Kate is also the creator of the Inspired Impact Book Series, which has published the titles: *Women Who Ignite, Women Who Inspire, Women Who Influence, Women Who Impact, Women Who Illuminate, Women Who Rise* and *Women Who Empower*.

Kate received her degree in Mass Communications and Interpersonal Communication Studies from Towson University, MD. After 10 years in the corporate industry, Kate decided it was time to fulfill her true passion. Kate then went on to study business at Wharton School of Business at The University Of Pennsylvania where she received her certificate in Entrepreneur Acceleration.

Kate now brings her expertise to mainstream media where she has been featured as the Mindset and Publishing expert on Fox 29, Good Day Philadelphia, HBO, in the Huffington Post and various other televisions, news and radio platforms.

To learn more about becoming an author in the Inspired Impact Book Series, or working with Kate directly on achieving your goals or publishing your book, including children's books, please visit her website at www.katebutlerbooks.com.

Kate would love to connect with you!

FB- @katebutlerbooks

IG- @katebutlerbooks

PERMISSION TO DO IT SCARED

AMY SHONKA

> " *When I stand before God at the end of my life, I would hope that I would not have a single bit of talent left, and could say, 'I used everything you gave me.'*"
> -Erma Bombeck

Have you thought about what you lose when you allow fear to keep you stuck?

Inside a seed of fear is opportunity—it's where change exists. I call these the "scary and exciting" moments. I am scared to make the change, but at the same time, the outcome can be so exciting!

In my own life, the "scary and exciting" moments show up all the time. Staying put is always an option, despite knowing the place I am living is no longer best for me. It is familiar. Familiar can be *comfortably uncomfortable*.

I remember this *comfortably uncomfortable* feeling 30 years ago. I started out doing exactly what I thought my family and society expected of me. I went to college, got married, got a "real" job. I started having my four amazing kids within a year of taking my vows. It was all *good*.

Well, I say *good* because I was in denial. I was ignoring my inner voice. The voice that said day after day, "You should start your own business." "You should leave this job that isn't fulfilling." "You should sell this house and raise your kids in the country."

I loved the thought of doing those things, but I wasn't actually doing any of them. I was, like so many of us, stuck and giving fear the final say.

"What if we cannot pay our bills?" "What if we lose the house?" "What if I regret the decision?"

Have you ever stayed stuck because change seems too difficult? We live with this inner argument vacillating between where we are and where we want to be.

Do you see this in yourself? Do you stay stuck in "good enough" because you are too scared to make it great? I sure did. However, when I look back at the times I ignored the fear and leapt anyway, I am so grateful I did it!

My first job out of college was working for a non-profit, coordinating the volunteers. I was driving an hour into the city through traffic for a low paying job. I remember being almost nine months pregnant, sitting at a red light in my little car at a clogged six-lane intersection, looking over at a busy daycare center. It was overcast that day and bone-chillingly cold. Yet, standing at the rusting eight-foot fence surrounding the center were a dozen kids. Their little fingers gripped the metal links as they watched and waited for their parents to pick them up. At that moment, I knew I had to find other work so I could be at home with my baby. Fear kicked in; could I accomplish that?

I had just graduated from college a year before, and here I was, already leaving the business world to try working from home. It seemed like an irresponsible thing to do. I had student loans and a degree for heaven's sake! I wrestled with it for a few weeks; then, I held my breath, walked into my boss' office, and resigned from my position. I faced my fears and headed home thinking, "I'll figure out how to make this work."

My first work from home job was painting pottery for a company that made personalized snack bowls. We lived on the first floor of a rundown home we were slowly renovating. We rented out our upstairs to an elderly couple to help pay the $640 monthly mortgage.

Each night after putting my infant daughter to bed, I'd paint from 9:00 p.m. to 2:00 a.m. in the hot and humid kitchen. The oven had to be on for hours to bake the pottery after it had been painted. That heat, coupled with the lack of air conditioning, sent the temperature in the kitchen soaring to a sticky 100 degrees or more. The $1.40 I made per item was slow to add up. I had no sick time and no vacation time, but that job helped me work from home which was important to me. I became a master at stretching a dollar to make ends meet. But, my "doing it scared" experiment seemed to be working. I was happy with my decision. In the decades since those days painting in my kitchen, my work has changed dramatically, but it was the first important step in becoming a successful business owner.

When our oldest child just had her first birthday, my husband and I agreed to watch our friend's six teenage foster boys for a weekend. We had a great time taking the boys hiking, and I loved cooking dinner for the nine of us.

Within a month, we started discussing becoming a foster family. Once again, I felt that fear and I had so many questions, "Will this work with our own child?" "What happens as we have more kids?" "Do we have enough space?" Ultimately, we decided to dive in and go through the licensing process. On a Thursday afternoon, I opened a letter which announced we were now an official foster family. That night, around midnight, the local police department called to ask if we could take in a three-year-old girl. She was the first of 84 foster children to move into our home over the next decade. It, too, was one of the best decisions we ever made.

When welcoming foster children into your home, you are working with kids who have experienced various hardships and traumas. Thankfully, we acknowledged our fear and did it anyway. Many of our foster children came to our home in the middle of the night with all of their worldly possessions stuffed in a black garbage bag, carried in by a helpful police officer. It was always a humbling experience to greet these kids at the back door where our aging and wise golden retriever helped ease the children's transition immediately.

We changed our family's lives for the better by diving right into foster parenting. Our own children spent 11 years learning to share their toys, their home, and their family with kids whose lives were in limbo. Our kids saw firsthand what it meant for a child to have nothing but the clothes on their back yet remain resilient and hopeful.

Watching our foster children blossom into curious, playful, joyous people was the greatest gift of the experience. Our whole family learned how to care for strangers until they felt like family. Taking in foster children wasn't always easy. Working with the biological parents was often challenging, as were the issues the children had due to their past trauma. Every time it was completely worth it.

A couple years into foster care, we began having more children of our own. The lifelong goal I had—building a home in the country to raise my family—kept rolling around in my mind. I would wake up in the morning, feeling bold and strong and think, "That's it! I am going to figure out a way to build this house and it will be incredible!" Five hours later, I'd be thinking, "Absolutely not! Why change what is fine?" In the end, I always came back to, "I can make this work."

Finally, we decided to raise the kids in the country. Going all-in on this decision was at once scary and so incredibly exciting. Years after finding land and building our home, I would sit on the big front porch, and think, "I am so glad we did this."

Our four kids are all grown up now. They consistently share that having foster siblings throughout their childhood made every day an exciting adventure. They regularly played as a group in the woods behind our house, rode horses around our property, and jumped on the trampoline for hours on end. We welcomed our foster children on family vacations and summer outings to a cabin in northern Minnesota. We felt strongly that our foster kids had one chance to create a memorable childhood, and our contribution was when they were with us. Our children willingly shared everything in their lives with their foster siblings throughout the whole process.

The decision to be a foster family, although filled with fear, just felt *right*. In hindsight, this intimidating choice was undeniably one of the best decisions we made for ourselves and our family. We had courageously stepped into a life that felt truly *good*.

Even in the midst of living a good life, we can get off track. Although I already had seven kids under my roof, a company I was running, and a busy spouse, I neglected to protect the pace of life I wanted for our family. As a result, life felt far too busy.

I said "yes" to too many things and created an overloaded lifestyle. It felt like I didn't have a choice to slow down. If you would have asked me how I was, I would have answered, "I'm good, just really busy."

By being too busy, I was unable to find time to lighten my load or focus on growth and opportunity. I talked about slowing down but was not acting on it. I wanted to create a business that would allow me to flow between home and work as needed, but I was challenged as to what that could be.

Forward progress is not always a straight line. There may be lots of starting, stopping, and U-turns, and that's perfect. For me, progress happened by taking baby steps toward fulfilling my vision and shifting along the way.

I slowly let go of other commitments, so the family had my attention. I sold off a business, acquired a yoga studio, and founded a life coaching company, both of which I still own and run today. I made changes that allowed my life to continue evolving.

As I have gotten older, my "doing it scared" moments haven't gotten any smaller.

I ended a marriage after 22 years. I bought and fully renovated a home on my own after I turned 40. I started businesses alone and grew them to impact others. Each step forward was preceded by acknowledging fear and thoughtfully taking action.

If you're scared to leave...

If you're scared to stay...

If you're scared to act...

It's likely you are on the edge of growth. This is the perfect time to face the fear and welcome yourself to the next stage of life.

I am yet again at a "do it scared" moment in my life. I want to allow my creativity to flourish in new ways again. I am focusing on helping people lighten the load of their life to experience more vibrancy and freedom and renovating spaces to help their homes feel amazing.

For me, making changes still feels scary—that hasn't gone away. I've gained skills over time and trust myself to figure it out, even when things don't go as planned. I have grown resilient, consciously moving forward over and over. My self-esteem is strong as a result of conquering fear, working through struggles, and seeing how capable and resourceful I am. Instead of just saying yes to everything that comes my way, I decide what I want my life to look like. I've learned to gracefully let go of the parts that don't fit inside that new vision.

What is the next step in *your* journey? What is just outside of your comfort zone that you cannot ignore any longer? How can you feel the fear, listen to your intuition, and take action? These are questions my clients have asked me for 15 years and below are my suggestions:

1. First, you need to get quiet. We live in a time where we are surrounded by noise and stimulation nearly 24 hours a day. Living in chaos doesn't allow adequate quiet for you to hear your inner voice.
   a. Wake up a few minutes early.
   b. Make your coffee or tea and sit down alone for 2-5 minutes each morning.
   c. Take a deep breath and simply be present with yourself.
      i. At first your mind will likely be busy hopping from one thought to the other. Allow this to happen.
      ii. After a few days you will start to feel calmer and will become more in tune to what your intuition is telling you.
      iii. Learn to listen for guidance from within yourself.
2. Spend time journaling what you are really thinking and feeling. Sometimes it's scary to actually say or write what you truly desire. When you practice freestyle journaling, you will get better at writing whatever comes to mind. By writing it out, you will begin to be more comfortable with thinking about it and ultimately, listening to it.
3. Start having conversations with yourself. The next time you have a decision to make:
   a. Ask yourself, "What do I really want to come from this?"
   b. If you cannot decide, try saying, "If I did know what to do, what would I do right now?"

    c. Also ponder "How do I want my life to feel? To look like?"

4. Ask yourself often: What can I let go of right now in order to slow down and simply listen? What has my inner voice been whispering to me?

Many of us have learned not to trust ourselves enough, often deferring our decisions to be made by others. Sometimes, we must be reminded: We have a deep soul with great wisdom. That wisdom reveals itself when we slow down and get quiet.

I have a quote that sits on my desk in my at-home office. I read it often. Perhaps it speaks to you and me both and will help you find the strength and permission to "do it scared".

"In the end, we only regret the chances we didn't take, the relationships we were afraid to have, and the decisions we waited too long to make."

-unknown

AMY SHONKA

Amy's expertise is in holistic living and as an organizational wellness specialist. As a speaker, author, and coach, Amy works with companies, colleges, and with awesome people to *Lighten the Load: how to thrive when you are stretched too thin*.

She is the creator of LifeRevamp, the owner of HeartWork Studio, and the founder and director of HeartWork Teacher Training School.

As an Amazon bestselling author, Amy created and published *The Back and Forth Journal, Simple Thoughts Press, 2006 (out of print)*, coauthored *Fashionably Late: Real Life Stories of (Finally) Showing Up!, Fashionably Late Productions, LLC, 2016*, and is a contributing author of *Permission Granted, Kate Butler Books, 2020*.

Amy enjoys life with her husband, four grown kids, and stepson. She is a former foster mom to 84 children. You can find out more about her at www.amyshonka.

"It's your responsibility to show the world how to treat you by the way in which you treat yourself."

LISA NICHOLS

PERMISSION TO BE A LIGHT
FOR THE WORLD

BRONWEN TALLEY-COFFEY

As I turn fifty, I am thinking about the people who have influenced my life and shaped me into the person I am today. I marvel at how I have rewoven the threads of my life, especially the broken ones, so that I can stand in my own power and accept myself—just as I am. Frankly, I am excited about the next fifty years because now I am in the driver's seat. I am the one who gets to decide who I am, where I am going, and who I want to become.

Growing up in the Blue Ridge mountains of Western North Carolina, I spent most of my time outdoors. Haywood County, nestled between several other counties, borders Tennessee. I spent my early years playing among the apple trees in Barber Orchard in Waynesville. In those days, children could play outside unattended, knowing that you better be in before supper. Running, playing

49

imaginary games, climbing trees, and riding bikes were the daily norm for most children. That's how it was for me. I was free to run and play, dreaming up adventures that would carry me from one day to the next.

My daddy was what they used to call a traveling salesman. He spent his work week driving a large box truck through the narrow, winding backroads of the mountains. He visited Mom-and-Pop country stores selling candy! For 37 years, my dad worked for Waynesville Candy Company and was known far and wide as The Candy Man.

I remember his work truck was like a child's dream. Boxes and boxes of candy lined the shelves in the back of that truck. It was filled with an array of chocolate bars, sweet, tart, and sour candies, chewing gums of all varieties, and lollipops of every shape and size!

Once a week, usually on Thursday, I got to climb up into that rolling candy store and choose one piece of candy. It was my treat, and I looked forward to it every week. It was a special day, and I was a happy child.

I always proclaimed to be a Daddy's girl. He seemed to take so much pride in me and I relished it. I missed him terribly when he was gone. I was usually up to see him off in the early mornings, but already tucked into bed late at night when he came home. I can still remember how hard he worked to provide what he could for our family.

My mother was an entrepreneur. Her love of dogs led her to open her own grooming business in the basement of our home. She was self-taught and very talented, especially when designing intricate patterns on poodles. As her business thrived, she opened her own shop in the small town of Clyde. She expanded her services to include dog training in obedience, and years later, she would add raising and showing standard poodles to her repertoire.

I was fortunate to have a mother who worked from home. She cooked meals, cleaned house, did the laundry, and mowed the lawn. On the weekends, we would have a picnic on the parkway, go camping in Cataloochee Valley, or take a special trip to Sears in Asheville. She made sure all the household chores were complete, in and out of the house, so we could have family time on the weekends.

Every year, in late May or early June, I anticipated the arrival of my Aunt Patsy from California. She was one of my mom's three older sisters. She would ride a Trailways bus into town and we would pick her up at the bus station. She would stay with my grandmother for a month before traveling back to California.

She was a delicate-framed woman with beautifully frosted hair and a genuinely soft, kind demeanor. She was always dressed in classic, understated fashions, polished off with kitten heels, and her earlobes held tiny sparkling earrings.

I looked forward to time spent shopping at Lay's dime store on Main Street in Waynesville, our annual visit to Biltmore Estate in Asheville, and the family fun days at Ghost Town in Maggie Valley and Santa's Land in Cherokee.

I admired my Aunt Patsy. Self-reliant, confident, and adventurous, Patsy had packed up and moved out west after graduating from business college. She made a home in California, had an amazing career, and never married. She was a self-made woman and, in my eyes, the picture of success. I wanted to be just like her.

51

My Grandmother Ella was a woman of few words, but her actions revealed the kind, loving person she was. Her stature was short and her frame a bit heavy. Her long, grayish hair was braided and wound around the top of her head, secured with a hairpin. She wore house dresses, some of which were handmade, and bedroom slippers with the toes cut out. She was happy being at home or working among the flowers in her yard. Once a month, she would have my mother drive her to the grocery store to shop.

It was my grandmother who had the most influence in my life. Grandma was my safe place—the place where I could be myself. I could laugh and be happy; I could be loud and carefree. I could play for hours or sit quietly, reading or watching television. We indulged in word searches and crossword puzzles. We would talk for hours about something or nothing at all. Whatever I did, as long as my grandmother was there, I was content.

The summer I turned seven, everything changed. In early September, my brother was born. I had prayed for a brother and was so excited when he arrived. The new wore off quickly as I began to realize I was no longer the only one getting attention. My time with my parents, which wasn't very much to begin with, was suddenly cut in half. I lost even more time when, as a toddler, my brother developed a medical condition. He required so much of my mother's care that I started feeling overlooked and alone.

And then came 1980. It was one of the worst years of my entire life. My sweet grandfather passed away in May. One night in June, during a thunderstorm, my dad backed the family station wagon over our long-haired gray kitten. The worst thing happened on my 10th birthday. Our house caught on fire and nearly everything we owned was destroyed.

After the house fire, I felt frightened and vulnerable. We'd lost our home, my favorite toys and stuffed animals were gone, and my clothes were hand-me-downs from people I didn't even know. The only things I had that were mine were the birthday presents I had just received—a new Barbie doll and a summer outfit.

We moved in with my grandmother. The unfortunate circumstances didn't change the fact that life goes on and bills need to be paid. Mom returned to her shop each day to groom dogs. Daddy continued to work during the week and spent every weekend rebuilding our home. Day by day our family struggled to reclaim all that we had lost.

The misfortunes kept coming. My brother caught the chickenpox and gave them to me. Our chickenpox gave Grandma a case of shingles. To add to the turmoil, my brother had one of his febrile convulsions and stopped breathing. My mom performed CPR while my grandmother called for an ambulance. I ran to the driveway to wave the EMT's toward the house.

My mother rode with my brother to the hospital while I stayed behind with my grandmother, waiting for news. She knew I was upset and worried. She never left me alone. I sat on the floor and played with my new Barbie doll as she sat and watched me. My grandmother assured me everything would be all right.

I loved living in my grandma's house. I can still see it in my mind. The small two-bedroom, one bath house had a detached garage and old horse barn down back. There were apple trees and a cherry tree with fruit perfect for cobblers and fried pies. A huge maple tree in the front yard provided a shady gathering spot for many conversations and lazy summer afternoons. There was a holly tree, a couple of elms, and another maple that had a rope swing for the kids to play on.

Throughout the year, birds would drop by for a rest in the trees or a meal from the bird feeder. Sparrows, finches, and cardinals were common visitors. The air was constantly filled with their songs. Occasionally, we would find a nest in one of the trees or bushes.

There were flowers galore! Oh, the colors of them all. Pastel yellow daffodils were plentiful in the spring around Easter. Every color of tulip you could possibly imagine would be blooming on the upper bank. Throughout the spring and summer, there were ruby red velvet sweetheart roses, white and pink snowball bushes, black and gold Black-eyed Susan's, blue hydrangeas, and purple irises. The stone wall running parallel to her driveway was overflowing with light pink, deep purple, white, and dark pink rock flowers. Monarch butterflies of orange and black would flutter from bush to bush. Honeybees made their way from the flowers to the clover on the lawn. By fall, two grape vines would be fragrant with heavy-hanging ripe fruit, perfect for juice and jelly.

My grandmother was an amazing cook. Even in her late seventies, she cooked three meals a day, every single day. It was important for her to be able to feed her family. I remember stories of how my grandmother would cook meals and take them to other relatives who didn't have as much. My grandmother would open her door to a stranger who had stopped to ask for a drink of water or something to eat. She would welcome them in, provide water or a meal, and bid them a safe journey. She never turned anyone away who asked for her help.

One of our relatives, Great Aunt Bessie, would come to visit. Her clothes were tattered and worn. She was disheveled and unkempt, and she had poor hygiene. Grandma would welcome her in, prepare a hot meal, invite her to enjoy a warm bath, wash her clothes, and let her take a nap or spend the night before she left for home.

I never heard my grandmother mutter a cross word or talk ill of anyone. She was an amazing example of kindness and acceptance, always putting others first. Her love and care helped me recover from the devastation I felt after our house burned down. She was my role model, my mentor, and my greatest strength.

In the years that followed, I started to discover the person I was to become. I took dance classes at a local studio. I enjoyed all forms of dance, but tap was by far my favorite. Years of dance workshops and competitions had prepared me for my big break in New York City as a Radio City Rockette. It was my dream, until I found out my height of 5'2" wasn't going to make the cut. There has always been something about me, something deep down that says if I can't be the best, move on to something else. So, I moved on.

As a teenager, I became interested in beauty pageants. Instead of the sparkly costumes of a Rockette, I dreamed of wearing stunning evening gowns. Unfortunately, my first pageant wasn't what I had dreamed of. Instead of an elegant evening gown, I wore a long poofy dress borrowed from my mother's friend. It was buttercup yellow and a bit outdated. I felt neither confident nor beautiful, so it was no surprise when I didn't place.

The next year, my grandmother gave my mom money to buy

a gown from a boutique uptown. It was satin with a sheer overlay and the color alternated in an ombre, from pink to blue. It was modern and elegant. Grandma wanted me to be as beautiful as she saw me. Her faith gave me the confidence I would need to win.

My tap routine, a classic number to *Boogie Woogie Bugle Boy*, was perfection. My interview left a bit to be desired. Of all the items listed on my questionnaire, three judges wanted to talk about the family goat, Easter. I smiled and made the best of it. I was so upset when I left the building, I vowed to kiss the goat if I won the pageant.

I rode on a float in the Christmas parade in front of the whole town that year as Young Miss Blue Ridge Valley. And, yes, I kissed that goat!

I have a picture of me sitting on the side of Grandma's bed in the dress she bought me. I wore it to my first dance. Grandma was very tired and stayed in bed most of the time. She was getting weaker, and I dreaded what I knew would eventually come. I grew scared of spending nights with my grandmother, as I often did. I was afraid the family would blame me if she died on my watch. The lesson I take away from that is to never deny yourself time with someone you love due to what others might think. If I had it to do over again, I would have stayed and made sure she knew she was not alone, just as she had done for me so many times before. I would have assured her that it would be all right, just as she did when they took my brother away in the ambulance.

Near the end, as she lay in the hospital bed unable to speak, I asked my Grandma if there was anything I could do for her. She shook her head, "No." There were so many things I wanted to say to her, but in my family, we didn't say those words out loud. Grandmothers have an uncanny ability to read a child's heart. She knew what was in mine. She took her oxygen mask away from her face, and looking into my eyes, she clearly said, "I love you."

My grandmother passed away that night. My mother sent me to school the next day because she had things to do. Word got around the school that my grandmother, my best friend, the only person who knew me better than I knew myself, had gone home to be with the Lord. I tried to be strong, but I cried. At the funeral home, a cousin told me not to cry, but I did. I remember looking at her in the casket—asleep, but I don't remember anything else about that day. I buried it all deep inside.

I do know that day was a turning point for me. I was 15 years old, and I was tired of people telling me what to do, how to feel, and what to think. I was my own person. I gave myself permission to choose who I wanted to be, what I wanted to believe, and to go out and make a difference in the world. I couldn't wait to finish high school and move on with my real life. I had so many things to accomplish.

Life doesn't always turn out the way that we dream it will. However, there are many things I have wanted to do that I have accomplished. I followed in my aunt's footsteps and began a career immediately out of high school. I continued my education and training to become a person of many trades. I found my niche in sales, mostly because of the connections I made with the people I met along the way. I never pushed a sale, and I had many potential clients return months and even years later to purchase a product from me. They often said they appreciated my kindness and understanding when they couldn't buy and wanted to reward me with the sale when they could.

I pursued my certification to become a training coach; and, like my mother did so many years before me, I launched my own business. My days are filled helping individuals create the best version of themselves, assisting businesses with customer service training and employee development, and helping nonprofit organizations with fundraising. The commonality with all three areas of my business are the people. It's all about the interaction: personal relationships with each other, company-to-employee dynamics, and fundraiser-to-donor connections.

I often said my daddy never met a stranger. He once told me to take the time to talk to those who might not have anyone else to talk to. In a nutshell, he believed you should help those you can and pray for those you can't.

My grandmother passed her secret to me all those years ago. It's the secret I teach today—the little things in life are really the big things. We should take the time to observe, acknowledge, and appreciate the people and the things around us. It's about seeing the person next to you and acknowledging them with a small act of kindness.

It brings me great joy to respect the dignity of everyone I meet and to realize that every life is just as valuable as my own. For me, it is easy to see the value in others. Whether I'm interacting with a waitress while eating in a restaurant, serving a meal at the local soup kitchen and speaking to the guests that come in, or visiting the animal shelter and interacting with a dog or cat, I am taking the time to see, hear, and acknowledge another life.

I am my grandmother made over, many times. I decided after she passed that I wouldn't let her spirit die with her. It carries on through me. I have an endless love for flowers, trees, birds, butterflies, and bees. I love warm spring days, hot summer mornings, crisp fall afternoons, and cold, snowy evenings. I look for the beauty and positive side in everything. I am thankful for family and grateful for good friends.

For me, the harder work is to extend the same kindness and love to myself. Just like many of us, I am prone to put everyone else first. Life is busy and there is only so much time in a day. I am learning that it is all right for me to extend that love and kindness to myself. Taking the time to love and appreciate myself helps me to better serve those around me.

My grandma taught me about unconditional love. My actions keep her memory alive. Love is like the flame of a candle. The more candles we light, the more light we make visible in the world. I'm giving myself permission to be the light I want to see in this world. That's what I'm going to do with my next fifty years.

BRONWEN TALLEY-COFFEY

Bronwen Talley-Coffey is a Motivational Speaker and Certified Trainer in the Success Principles and Canfield Methodology. She is the owner of Aspire Training & Development, LLC, located in her hometown of Waynesville, North Carolina.

With over 30 years in sales and public relations, she is an expert in customer service and sales training, as well as an award-winning sales recruiter. Her passion is helping others achieve their highest potential, both personally and professionally.

Bronwen is a Paul Harris Fellow with Rotary International. She was named a 2017 Woman of the Year by the National Association of Professional Women. She serves on the board for FUR of WNC, a nonprofit organization dedicated to helping cats in need. Bronwen is a facilitator for her local Goal Friends group, whose purpose is to help women create their own roadmap to reach individual goals.

Bronwen grew up in the mountains of Western North Carolina. She spent thirteen years living in upstate South Carolina before returning to her mountain home. She lives on her ranch with her family, two dogs, seven cats, and four horses, all of which are rescue animals. She enjoys the beauty of nature, reading and reflecting, and spending quality time with friends.

www.AspireTrainingDevelopment.com

PERMISSION TO GRIEVE

SAMANTHA RUTH

I wrote a different chapter for this book. And I hated it!! It's the only time I've ever struggled while writing. I think I wanted to will away my grief. It's such a large part of my story... but it is exactly that—just one part. There's so much more, and I want to share those stories.

I am where I am. Just last week, I had a meltdown. Ok... a Major meltdown!! And I realized that I STILL need to give myself permission to grieve. Almost two years after losing Jim and I still have to consciously remind myself that it's okay to be a mess and to grieve my way.

We live in this fast-paced world where googling is more common than being active. People talk about what's for dinner the minute after walking out of a funeral. Drive throughs. Fast Food Instant gratification. Delivery anything. It's no wonder that slowing down can be difficult. It almost feels like it's frowned upon.

Grief changes you. In so many ways. My brain just works at a new, slower pace. Things that used to be a breeze can take me hours to complete now. Reading. Processing. It's all new to me again.

Once I accepted this, it became much easier to live with my grief and to function. I stopped expecting things to be how they've always been because they'll never be that way again. I'll never be that Sam again.

I'm a new Sam and not by choice. At a retreat a few weeks ago, someone commented about me being a quiet person. Ha! Me! If only they knew. But, it's true. I have become quiet. (I've since been told that "I'm coming out of my shell." Phew!!) I'm getting back to that silly, goofy part of myself. I miss silly Sam. But, it takes conscious effort. I'm always acutely aware of my behavior and of recognizing new pieces of myself while still digging for some of the old pieces.

Losing my soulmate was like a nuclear bomb exploding inside of me and all around me. I was blown to bits. I'm still picking up the pieces. And, there's no time frame—no how-to manual. In my opinion, it will never get easier or go away. It just gets different, but it's Always Present.

Being in the presence of a grieving, hurting person makes people uncomfortable. They want to fix things—make them better. For me, that actually made everything worse. I was reminded of that during my meltdown. I was fighting the tears and doing my damndest to function. That's what we're taught, right? Put on a happy face. Fake it until you make it. Shake it off.

Honestly, that makes things a million times worse. When I allow myself to have the meltdown instead of fighting it, that's when I can breathe. Barely, but it's there—just enough to give me that glimmer of hope.

Why does society tell us to stuff it? More importantly, why do we listen??? I've always had that little voice, that gut feeling. We all do, but we aren't taught to listen to it!! I'm here to tell you to listen to it!!

Life without listening is like a tornado. It's literally going against what we know and feel... like swimming against the tide. Simply put—out of alignment.

I had been living out of alignment for as long as I can remember. Sometimes, I knew it was happening. I remember being really upset with my mom once. (Ok, busted. More than once). But, on this particular occasion, I was really hurt and didn't want to see her until I was in a better mindset.

"Just do it for me," my dad asked, and that was all it took.

Did the world end? No, but I was angry with myself for not listening to me!!

Other times, I wasn't aware of it at all. Like after losing Jim. I'm telling you, I literally felt like an infant. People told me when to eat. What to eat. When to sleep, not that I actually slept.

I couldn't function. I had to learn everything all over again. And things I'm not great at, like technology, sent me into instant overwhelm. Making decisions?? Nearly impossible. But, I just plugged along, going through the motions, surviving. Going through the motions. Surviving.

Meanwhile, my emotions were like that tornado, all over the place, wreaking havoc. I started getting unsolicited advice. You should get back to work. You should take off your wedding ring. You should get out more.

Thankfully, my mouth didn't say what my brain was thinking. Still, I started getting upset by comments like this. I started to feel the pressure of other people's expectations.

That's the little voice. The gut feeling. I realized that I needed to pay attention. My body was telling me something. I started to really see all of the clues. So, I made a decision. By myself. I decided to go to the mountains for our anniversary. Just me and my fur baby girl, Sassy—and my Success Principles book. As is true of any decision we make in life, people had opinions.

Most thought this was a horrible idea, at least the "going by myself" part. Only this time, it was different. I did not care one iota what anyone thought. I was being called to the mountains, and I listened to my "little voice" without questioning or overthinking.

You know what happened once I did exactly what my gut told me? I felt free. Free to live life on my terms. Free to trust myself. Free to grieve my way. Free to make decisions without caring what others think. Free. And, I decided in that instant that I never wanted to feel anything other than free again.

So, I gave myself permission. Permission to be myself, to get through things my own way, in my own time. And I realized I've had the permission all along. I was waiting for someone else to give it to me, and all I had to do was stand up and take it!!

The same is true for you!! I'm not saying it's easy. I still have my meltdowns. The mean girls in my head still try to convince me that I'm not good enough. But, I tune them out. I don't fight the meltdowns because that only makes it worse. Instead, I embrace them.

I look at them as gifts allowing me to release something that clearly needs to be released.

I am saying I came home from the mountains, and I started creating the life that I want. I got a puppy, Dallas. She brought joy back into our house, and she helped Sassy heal which has been the biggest gift of all. Getting Dallas was a decision many thought was crazy, but it was another one of my best decisions.

I continued listening to my body and to that little voice. I gave myself permission to heal, my way, and I devoted 2019 to myself and my healing. It was another decision that wasn't well received and another one of my best decisions–Ever.

Listening to and following my little voice is how I began to heal, something I honestly didn't believe was possible even six months ago. Trust me when I say that grieving is a personal journey. Your journey is different than mine. What we have in common is the right to grieve our own way. Permission Granted!!

SAMANTHA RUTH

Are you feeling overwhelmed? Lost? Stuck? Alone? Maybe even Helpless? I have visited all of those places, and I know how you feel. My name is Samantha Ruth and I am here to help you and your family.

I'm a Transformational Psychologist & Coach, and I help people by guiding them to live their best life—as their true self. I have the tools and heart-centered teachings, not only based on my education but from my own life experiences. I have been there, in rough, puzzling places, many times and come out on the other side. If other methods or professionals didn't work for you, let's chat and see how we can pick up your pieces and get you unpuzzled.

After practicing for more than 16 years, I moved to Colorado to marry my soulmate. I left clients who continued requesting my services, and I followed my intuition and created my online business. My mission is to change the way the world views mental health. In pursuit of this mission, I continue impacting lives through my books, keynote speeches, live events, and coaching programs. Connect with me to see what's the best fit for you!

www.samantharuth.com
www.samantharuth.com/assessment
https://www.facebook.com/samanthamruth/

"Never underestimate the power of planting a seed."

KATE BUTLER

PERMISSION TO LIVE
YOUR PURPOSE

LINDSAY SMITH

It was a warm, sunny day in July, and I was 16 years old. I was volunteering at Sacred Heart Community Center's Academic Day Camp in downtown San Jose, California. We worked with elementary and middle school students from the lowest socioeconomic neighborhoods to support them in gaining the skills they needed to be successful in the upcoming school year. I loved it. I loved seeing their smiles as the kids learned new skills and hearing the pride in their voices as they began believing in themselves and their abilities.

Jose was one of these students. He was 12 years old and was kind, playful, and had a wonderful sense of humor. He also came from a broken home, lived in a gang infested neighborhood, and sometimes struggled to have his basic needs met. Unfortunately, joining a gang around his age felt like the only option for many in

69

his neighborhood.

On this day in July, Jose confided in me that after camp that day, he was going to participate in a knife fight that would serve as his initiation into the gang. I knew what a significant impact this choice would have on his life from that point forward and I didn't want him to go. After multiple discussions and efforts to persuade him not to go, I proposed a trade. If he chose not to go to the knife fight that day and gave me his knife, then I would, using my savings from my job that summer, take him to a fancy lunch at the Fairmont hotel.

Jose had never been inside this luxurious hotel, much less eaten there. He was intrigued by the idea, and I think a little relieved to have a way out of the fight. He decided to spend the afternoon having lunch with me at the Fairmont instead of participating in the gang initiation. We spent the lunch talking about his future and his potential. We talked about how every choice he makes will either lead him closer to or further from his goals.

Jose did not join the gang that summer. His choice that day led him to see that he didn't have to follow the same path as his peers. He wanted more for himself, and that day he gave himself permission to move toward his goals. I learned so much through this experience with Jose. I learned that I could empower someone to see other options, to make better choices, and to see their own worth and potential. My time with Jose allowed me to see that I could truly make a difference.

Driven To Make A Difference

I was so inspired by Jose that I went on to become a Licensed Clinical Social Worker, working with teens in schools, group homes, foster homes, and juvenile hall. Eventually, I started Teen Therapy Center, my first psychotherapy practice. I was able to utilize my entrepreneurial skills as I supported the emotional development of teens and I loved it! I loved being the light and holding hope for these teens until they could do this for themselves, until they could see their own worth, value, and abilities. I poured all I had into making a difference for my clients and the community.

Soon, my business was thriving, and I was hiring other therapists to work with me. As I started managing my new team members, I learned very quickly that I was an awful boss. I was an extreme micromanager. I didn't consider my team members' strengths or passions. I just wanted them to do exactly what I did. I created a horrible environment that was not conducive to my team members' happiness or to retention.

I knew things had to change. I dug in and learned what I could through books, seminars, and trial and error. As I learned more about what it meant to manage people, I encouraged each person to identify what they loved doing and to incorporate their passion into their work.

One therapist loved the outdoors, so she started incorporating walks into her sessions. As she did this, her clients began opening up more. They would share things with her on their walks that they hadn't previously shared. Her clients saw the changes they wanted happening faster as they began opening up more. The therapist loved this time she got to spend outside, and she was excited by the rapid progress her clients made. Not only was she so much happier coming to work each day, she became a more effective therapist.

Our culture began to shift. Team members enjoyed coming to work, and they began encouraging and supporting each other. It was a whole new environment that people loved being part of. This showed me that not only could I make a difference in the lives of my clients, but I could also make a difference in the lives of my team members. I loved seeing them shine as they gave themselves permission to live their purpose. When my team members were living their purpose, so was I; together, we made an even more substantial impact in the lives of our clients.

Always Growing

As we made these changes and reached a new status quo, Teen Therapy Center continued to grow steadily—and I got the itch. You know the itch I'm talking about? The feeling where things are great, but you want to do more. Where some kind of growth or expansion or new product or service is just itching to come out. Where you want to create and serve in a new way. That's what I was feeling.

So, I opened my second therapy center, Family Therapy Center, where we started working with families, children, adults, and couples. I loved growing both of these centers while continuing to provide therapy myself. I felt like I was making a difference in the lives of my clients, with my team members, and in the community.

Each time my team and I created a new service, program, or center, it lit me up. I loved creating, innovating, finding new ways to serve our populations and make a difference in their lives. I loved growing—both personally and professionally. Sometimes people would ask me, "Why can't you just be satisfied with how it is?" or "Are you done now?" And it wasn't that I wasn't content. I was content. I was filled with joy and deeply grateful for all I had accomplished and for what I got to do on a daily basis. I just wanted to do more and to help more.

I will always choose to be in a state of growth. This desire does not come from a lack or an emptiness, it comes from a place of fullness and of love. It comes from knowing I am meant to make a difference. Every single one of us has unlimited potential. Once we reach a goal, we get to dig deep inside and discover another layer to our gifts, we get to continue growing as we unlock our next level of potential. The more we push ourselves, the more we grow, and the bigger difference we can make—in our families, in our companies, in our communities, and in our world.

So, as both Teen Therapy Center and Family Therapy Center continued to grow and thrive, I looked for the next way that I could grow and make a difference. The answer came in the form of a game. A card and dice game focusing on topics like family, friendship, self-esteem, stress, values, and feelings that therapists could use in therapy and that parents could play with their teens at home to effortlessly open up communication.

It took about 13 months to turn *Talk About It!*® into a reality. During this time, I became acutely aware of two factors that influenced my ability to reach my goals and to make the difference I was looking to make. The first was a combination of accountability and support. I shared my goals with anyone who would listen which kept me committed. I worked with an accountability partner who was as committed to me achieving my goals as I was. I had people in my life who supported me, encouraged me, and believed in my vision.

The second factor was working 1:1 with a high-level coach. My coach was with me every step of the way—pushing me, helping me to see things I couldn't, and encouraging me to dream bigger, think bigger, and play bigger. My coach also showed me the importance of becoming crystal clear about my life purpose. I'd known since that first summer working with Jose that I was meant to make a difference, that I was meant to help people, but I hadn't put a lot of thought into it beyond that.

Clarified Purpose

Once I grasped the importance of clarifying my purpose, I spent time meditating, journaling, sitting with God, listening to Him, and asking for direction and clarity. I thought about my true passions and desires. What do I love doing? What lights me up and makes it so I can't wait to get out of bed in the morning? I took an inventory of the things I was good at. I spent time contemplating the difference I wanted to make in the lives of those around me. Who did I most want to impact? Why was it important to me?

It became clear that I loved to inspire people, to empower them to feel good about themselves and to make a difference—in their own lives and in the lives of others. But how did I communicate this? What did I want them to feel? I began to receive a series of words in response to my questions—words like joyful, worthy, significant, loving, and confident. Although I was getting clear answers to my questions, it wasn't feeling 100% right for me. So, for weeks I continued to sit with and meditate on these questions. I was committed to being in the process of my purpose unfolding. And one day it did. God made my purpose clear to me.

I am meant to empower people to truly love themselves, know their value, and believe in their abilities to achieve their highest visions—to make their difference, whatever that looks like for them. I felt deep within myself that this is what I am meant to do. I struggled for decades to know that I am lovable, valuable, and capable—especially to truly love myself. Those years prepared me for this purpose, and I was ready. In fact, I had been living out my purpose for many years, but now was ready to do it with more clarity and focus.

I knew that I had been living my purpose through providing 1:1 therapy and through the culture I created with my teams and the way I ran my centers, but now I wanted to make a difference on a bigger scale. The creative itch was back!

Making A Bigger Difference

When I first contemplated making a bigger difference, I immediately assumed it would be with teenagers. However, as I thought more about it, I realized that for teens to truly love themselves, know their worth, and believe in their abilities, it's best if they begin learning these things as children. Then I realized that for children to internalize these concepts, the adults in their lives must believe these things, be living them out in their own lives, and be modeling them for their children.

So, using everything I'd learned in years of providing therapy and participating in transformational growth workshops, I created a personalized online course for adults that empowers the users to love themselves more, to know their worth and value, to discover or clarify their purpose, and to believe in their abilities to live out their purpose and make their difference—essentially to be their best self.

It soon became clear that the need for this program was even bigger than I first envisioned, so in addition to being offered to individuals, this program is now also offered to corporations. Through this program each individual team member, led by their CEO, experiences profound transformations in their personal and professional lives and enormous progress toward their goals. The entire team is propelled forward to reaching the company's highest vision faster, in more creative ways, and with a determined passion. Each individual and the company as a whole begin making a bigger difference.

Because the truth is that each one of us can make a difference. You can make a difference. You have a purpose. You are lovable. You are valuable. You are capable of achieving and exceeding your highest vision. You deserve to always be growing, unlocking your unlimited potential, to reach heights higher than your highest dream, and to make the difference you were meant to make.

When you give yourself permission to love yourself, you end up acknowledging your value, which allows you to believe in your abilities and make a bigger difference. This is when we know our life is on purpose, your purpose. I know you can do it, and more than anything I know you deserve it.

Are you feeling over-whelmed? Lost? Stuck? Alone? Maybe even Helpless? I have visited all of those places, and I know how you feel. My name is Samantha Ruth and I am here to help you and your family.

I'm a Transformational Psychologist & Coach, and I help people by guiding them to live their best life—as their true self. I have the tools and heart-centered teachings, not only based on my education but from my own life experiences. I have been there, in rough, puzzling places, many times and come out on the other side. If other methods or professionals didn't work for you, let's chat and see how we can pick up your pieces and get you unpuzzled.

After practicing for more than 16 years, I moved to Colorado to marry my soulmate. I left clients who continued requesting my services, and I followed my intuition and created my online business. My mission is to change the way the world views mental health. In pursuit of this mission, I continue impacting lives through my books, keynote speeches, live events, and coaching programs. Connect with me to see what's the best fit for you!

www.samantharuth.com
www.samantharuth.com/assessment
https://www.facebook.com/samanthamruth/

PERMISSION TO FOLLOW
YOUR DESTINY

MARCI SHIMOFF

Granting myself permission has been a lifesaver for me as well as the ticket to an amazing career that I'm beyond grateful for.

Over the course of my journey, I've been able to grant myself permission in two critical ways: taking care of myself and listening to my soul.

During the past 35 years, I've traveled more than three million miles around the world speaking and teaching, and if I hadn't given myself permission to take great care of myself, I wouldn't have survived! Taking care of myself goes against my grain as I was conditioned, like so many women are, to take care of everyone else first. But I've found that giving myself permission to prioritize self-care is the least selfish thing I can do, since it's the only way I can effectively serve others.

79

The other really important way I give myself permission is to listen to and follow my soul's wisdom.

Early in my career, I had a coach who taught me a three-step formula for success in manifesting what I want (I love it because it rhymes):

--Intention: Be clear about what you want to create

--Attention: Put your thoughts, words, feelings, and actions behind it

--No Tension: Let go, be in ease, relax, and trust.

Most people are really good at one of these steps, okay at one, and not great at one—and it's that last step they need to work on. For me, the "no tension" step has been my life lesson. Here's how this has played out for me.

My intention for my career became clear to me when I was 13, and I had a powerful vision that I'd spend my life speaking around the world, inspiring thousands of people at a time to live their best lives. I *knew* that was my destiny. My parents weren't very happy about that since they'd never heard of a career as a speaker, and they'd encouraged me to be a dental hygienist, instead. Even so, my mom joked that I sure talked enough, so I might as well get paid for it. Ultimately, they encouraged me to follow my soul.

I put a lot of attention on making that vision a reality—I studied hard, got my MBA, was trained by some of the best speakers in the world, and paid my dues as a "road warrior" traveling from city to city delivering training programs on a grueling schedule. Though I was working really hard, I had reached a plateau, and I was totally burned out. I was "failing" at no tension.

Noticing my stressed state, a dear friend of mine said, "Marci, you need a break. You're coming with me on a seven day silent meditation retreat." I thought she was crazy! After all, I was a speaker, and I didn't *do* silence, nor did I think I had seven days free to just sit and do "nothing." But she was very convincing, so I listened to my inner guidance that knew she was right, and off I went.

The first few days were miserable. I was fidgety and impatient and couldn't wait for the week to be over. However, by the fourth day, I had settled down and was really enjoying the ease and no tension. While in a deeply relaxed state in the middle of a meditation, it was as though a lightbulb went off in my head, and I saw the words "Chicken Soup for the Woman's Soul." Immediately I knew I'd just been given a gift from the universe!

At the time there was only the original *Chicken Soup for the Soul* book, and nobody had thought of "specialty books." I saw that this was the way I'd be fulfilling the vision of my destiny that I'd had at 13.

There was only one problem: There were still three more days of silence! I'd just had the greatest epiphany of my life, and I couldn't tell anyone my idea!

The moment the retreat was over, I ran to the closest pay phone, (this was in the prehistoric days before cell phones) and called Jack Canfield, the originator of *Chicken Soup for the Soul*, whom I'd worked with on other projects. With great excitement, I said, "Jack, I've got it—*Chicken Soup for the Woman's Soul*." He responded with, "Wow! Great idea—no one has ever thought of that." He called the publisher, who also loved the idea, and 1½ years later my first book came out and immediately went to #1 on the *NY Times* bestseller list. That led me to write eight more books that have sold more than 16 million copies in 33 languages worldwide and speaking to audiences around the globe.

All of this was a direct result of giving myself permission to go on that seven day silent retreat and move into a state of no tension.

I believe we each have a soul destiny. I was fortunate to connect with my destiny when I was young. But it was only after I gave myself permission to take care of myself, to listen to my soul, and to follow my destiny that my dreams came true.

MARCI SHIMOFF

Marci Shimoff is a #1 New York Times bestselling author, a world-renowned transformational teacher and an expert on happiness, success, and unconditional love.

Her books include the NY Times bestsellers Happy for No Reason, Love for No Reason, and six titles in the Chicken Soup for the Woman's Soul series. With total book sales of more than 16 million copies worldwide in 33 languages, Marci is one of the bestselling female nonfiction authors of all time.

Marci is also a featured teacher in the film and book sensation, The Secret, narrator of the award-winning movie Happy, and host of the PBS TV show called Happy for No Reason.

Marci delivers keynote addresses and seminars on happiness, success, empowerment, and unconditional love to Fortune 500 companies, professional and non-profit organizations, women's associations and audiences around the world.

Marci is currently leading a one-year mentoring program called Your Year of Miracles. Her opening seminar has been heard by more than 200,000 people.

Marci earned her MBA from UCLA and holds an advanced certificate as a stress management consultant. She is a founding member and board member emeritus of the Transformational Leadership Council, a group of 100 top transformational leaders.

Through her books and her presentations, Marci's message has touched the hearts and rekindled the spirits of millions of people throughout the world. She is dedicated to helping people live more empowered and joy-filled lives.

www.HappyForNoReason.com

"You teach people how to treat you."

PATTY AUBERY

PERMISSION TO BE AUTHENTIC

JULI FACER SCARBROUGH

I want you to see me. Really see me, not just the blouse, the happy couple, or the real estate advertisements—I want you to see me for who I really am.

Have you ever wanted that before? Wanted the person you called on for help to truly understand your needs? Wanted the person who's asking questions to sincerely listen to your responses? Wanted the person who says they can help you to take the time to connect and see past the first impression?

I did. I was there. So, here I am wanting you to see me, transparent and authentic.

At first glance, you'll see that I am a part of a husband and wife real estate team, but as you look closer, you'll realize that we are so much more. My husband Brett and I have a real estate company, and we used to be all business. I like to call it "Life before conscious business" when we were craving to build our empire at any expense. Our attitude, commendably, was "we will do whatever it takes." My husband and I were working hard in our business. After several years in real estate, we were feeling very enslaved to our business. I felt like I worked all the time, like a hamster in a wheel, and it had become burdensome.

We had worked really hard, but I still felt like our brand and marketing were too generic and not something that either of us identified with, which made it feel phony, and I don't do phony. I felt we didn't approach the business with authenticity, making sure that all aspects of the business and messaging were true to us. We just went with the flow and did what all of the other real estate agents were doing. We even dressed like the other agents, rather than creating our own personal style. I felt like I had lost myself, like we had lost ourselves, and I really wanted that feeling of authenticity back.

I would fall asleep exhausted and then wake up a few hours later tossing and turning, running through every possible scenario about what could go wrong, and how I would fix it. I rarely saw my kids. My marriage was struggling, our business was taking all of the focus, and our own personal issues would go unresolved. I was experiencing outward success and yet was feeling very empty inside.

Brett and I had just won some production awards and were getting some positive attention at work, and I just wasn't really enjoying it. I would get attention for doing "well" and I just couldn't connect with the success. I was also having trouble connecting with my clients which is what I loved about the business in the first place. The joy that comes with understanding another person's needs and filling those needs is what fed my soul. Since I wasn't connecting with my clients, it was difficult to understand their needs and to be of true assistance.

As 2014 was coming to a close, it was the most successful year of my life, and I was completely burned out. I was exhausted. My health was suffering because I was sitting in the office for long stretches and not exercising enough. Brett and I were growing farther apart. I had to figure out another way to do life or I was going to lose the life I'd built for myself. I knew that the way I was going about it was not sustainable.

This was my aha moment, I needed to connect, I needed to feed my soul. So, I took time, and used it for myself. I didn't know where to turn, so I searched self-development and came across an event called "Breakthrough to Success." I was attracted to its claim that I could discover "my full potential"—MY full potential. My authentic self liked the sound of that. As I started to peel back all of the layers of programming and get down to who I was as an individual, I realized that I had created a character/facade and uncovering the "Real Juli" was my goal.

During the "Breakthrough to Success" event, we met a lot of the assistants and listened to them talk about their businesses. I could recognize they were being truly authentic. I learned about conscious business. This phrase is used to recognize living your life based on knowing that everything is interconnected, finding your passions, and expressing values through your work. Conscious businesses seek to promote the intelligent pursuit of happiness in all its stakeholders. My soul was being fueled along with my mind.

We also got in touch with our marketing messages. Our marketing suggested we were very self-serving and ego-based, not at all focused on how we can help the customer. We were even wearing clothes in our business photos that we would never wear. We had created very convincing multi-tiered characters. With this new awareness, I realized that every detail of our business had to be authentic. We could do better, and this was the first step.

My heart was finally back in the right place—I could feel it. I had an epiphany. I was so focused on the end result that my heart was being skipped over, my clients' hearts were being left on the table, and I vowed to make the connection, the soul connection from that day forward.

I had wanted to be seen as a success, but not at the expense of myself. I needed to show up for me and for my clients.

Today, when I meet new potential clients, my first objective is to find out how I can help them. When I meet with them, I assume we will be working together, and I imagine us successfully finishing the process. I know that in the end, we will have the clients' familiarity and connection, and I bring the energy of that connection into that very first meeting. This allows me to be much more honest and genuine with them, and in turn, they are able to be more forthcoming and sincere with me. Building a relationship with them from the inception allows me to help them more effectively. Being more person-centric and approaching our client interactions with this automatic soul connection is so fulfilling to the "real Juli."

And, if it was important for me to be my authentic self, then of course I needed to reflect and ensure all the facets of my business mirrored that authenticity. How did I do that? Instead of saying, "How many houses did you sell?" We prefer to say, "How many people did you help move?" Instead of saying, "How much money did you make?" We ask, "How many of your customers gave you a five-star review?" One of the most crucial components of our business success is customer reviews. I find that if I begin a new relationship knowing that I am going to be asking for a five-star review at the end, I treat the whole process with more care and attention. I have shifted all the language in our office to be focused on the customer and to have full respect and gratitude for them.

Today some of my very best friends and vendors have come from past client relationships. When I opened up the business to new possibilities, I created a huge network of friends and colleagues in my community.

When I truly gave myself permission to be authentic by looking in the mirror and deciding that I am going to be real and live a happy life, I did not have to choose between "Being successful" OR "Being in a happy marriage." I did not choose between "Being a good Mom" OR "Being wealthy." Today, I give myself permission on an ongoing basis to connect within to what is really true for me, and what is the most authentic and true choice that I can make in every moment.

Now, business looks and feels as if I work for and with an amazing group of friends. I am able to approach new clients and new situations with so much confidence, knowing they are supported by a business that truly cares about them. The "burn out' that I felt in the past isn't a factor, as all of my clients are energizing for me, they no longer drain me like before. Each client relationship is based on authenticity, so I can really focus on helping them accomplish their goals. This is who I am, The Real Juli!

JULI FACER SCARBROUGH

Juli is an award-winning business owner and entrepreneur, working alongside her husband and business partner Brett Scarbrough. Juli and Brett help their clients to achieve new heights through working with them in their Real Estate and Coaching businesses. Over the past fifteen years, Juli has helped 800+ families to successfully move forward with their plans. She is tenacious and passionate with her service. Her clients will tell you, Juli is committed to achieving her clients' goals.

www.juliandbrett.com

PERMISSION TO BE FREE

CHERYL HOWELL

" *I remember thinking who is going to take care of my kids when I am dead?*

Am I really going to die today?"

It's true; a thousand things go through your mind when you face the possibility of death. My thoughts were about my children. *How did my life get to this point?* It is a surreal moment. The events are happening to you, but you feel like a bystander simply observing what is unfolding. It is in a moment like this that you are seemingly caught between two worlds. *Where were all my childhood dreams now? Did anything ever matter in my life? What's next?* This is my story. I would like to answer some of these questions. It is my sincere desire that in sharing my journey, someone will be inspired to give themselves permission to change, to speak out, or to alter their lifestyle in a way that will result in complete freedom and transformation.

In the fall of 1958, a baby was born to older parents. I wasn't a mistake—because there are no mistakes, but for many years I felt like a mistake. My parents were older folks and were now starting over with a baby. I was the "talk" of the family. Questions loomed as to why these two people wanted to start over with a baby after having grown children from previous marriages. The answer to that question was "they didn't".

After I was born, my grandmother moved next door and primarily raised me. She was my caregiver and protector. She did the best she could to give me a sense of belonging. She had a difficult life and worked hard for everything she had…which wasn't much. My parents drank a lot, especially my dad. They worked odd 12 hours shifts at work, and we lived about 20 miles from our little town. It was a lonely childhood. My grandmother was there for me; she was always working at something. She cared for me, but there were few "kid" like conversations. Her generation knew one thing…work. So, she took care of all my physical needs, cooked food I liked, and tended to duties of a daily household.

There were not many children who lived near me until I was about 9 years old. It was lonely spending most of my childhood by myself. My dad did not like me having anyone over to our house. I never really understood the reason why he didn't like having kids stay overnight.

My dad had his moments of being paternal; he also had his darker moments. He was very verbally and emotionally abusive. I only remember one incident of sexual abuse. I never wanted to remember any more incidents. There were clues; I didn't want to explore the signs. During this time, my mom was totally disengaged from her parental role. My grandmother was my rock.

I'm not sure what age the abuse began. My dad liked me more than my mom did. They fought all the time. My mother had no maternal instincts, and my dad was controlling. You never knew when he would erupt. I can't remember my exact age when I requested my own bedroom. I slept with my dad, and my mom had her own bedroom. They finally let me have my room. There was always this innate sense of "something not quite right" with all of this. I established a strong sense of knowing that boundaries were being crossed at an early age.

I lived in fear most of my life. I experienced an abnormal amount of anxiety in my early teens. I became obsessive/compulsive with my behavior. So many things I considered normal were so grossly abnormal. I had fears concerning everything…the weather, being abandoned, or simply making my dad angry. I can remember in the springtime when everything was coming to life that I would be crouched on the floor by my bed worrying about a tornado blowing us away. For years, even when I became an adult, when one beautiful white cloud would enter the sky, I began worrying that the storms were forming. I feared those beautiful white clouds would become severe storms.

I had tremendous issues with obsessive compulsive disorder (OCD). I had physical behaviors that I performed that were essential in order for me to feel peace. It was OCD at its worst. Looking back on that time, I feel so sorry for that little girl. I have gone back often over the years to comfort her. To an outsider looking at our family, life seemed good at our house. How fortunate I was to be an only child to older parents who seemingly doted on her. Unfortunately, what was *normal* for that little girl was to be afraid.

I realize now that my childhood made me insecure. It caused me to develop behavior that I could control…like the OCD habits. It also made me anxious and extremely self-conscious. I had no self-esteem and always looked for ways to blend with my friends. I always felt different and longed to feel normal. I saw my friends' parents and wished I had that structure in my home. I even made rules for myself so I could feel acceptable. I lacked the skills to connect with people. I wanted to please people. I could adapt to anything if everyone in my world was happy. I was simply trying to find ways to be accepted.

At 15, I met a guy that I thought would save me from this life. Little did I know, he was just a different version of my dad. My dad did not like that we dated. My mom loved him because he was a "Christian." She felt he would make my life perfect. I was 15 and seriously incapable of making any rational decision about a life partner and for God's sake—I was 15. Now that I'm a mother of two kids, I am mortified to think my daughter would date some guy and be considering marriage at 16. But that is what happened to me, and my mom went right along with it. I always felt she wanted me out of the house. She might have a chance to finally be with my dad alone. My dad, on the other hand, just voiced his disapproval and went about his business. It was as if I had chosen someone over him. and he was more than done with me.

I ended up marrying this guy at 16 and turned 17 two months later. In the state where I lived, you had to have at least one parent give permission to marry at that age. My mom gave permission without any hesitation. It is funny the name of this book is "Permission Granted." The "permission" my mom gave me forever changed my life. My dad seemed to "divorce" me at that time.

What I didn't know was that everything I was trying to escape would multiply in spades when I got married. I traded one master for another. From day one, my life became one of disappointment. This idea of "happily ever after" became "miserable now and forever after." My cultural teaching was to never divorce. So, when things began to disintegrate, ending the marriage never entered my mind. I had endured my childhood, now I had to endure my adulthood.

There was nothing "normal" about my marriage. My spouse was egocentric and narcissistic. His behavior was different than the normal person. However, because he had authority, somehow all the strange differences about him were OK. It was OK to not have sex when dating because "that would be sin". But he could put his hands all over my body and insist I touch him. Ironically, that behavior was justified. The sexual deviance was passed off as teenage desire. The sexual abuse I'd suffered did not leave me with a proper filter to distinguish between right and wrong behavior. So, all the lines were blurred between religious piety and sexual gratification. I grew more and more depressed over the years.

I couldn't see that this pattern was going to be fixed with marriage; it became worse with marriage. In conservative religious circles, marriage gives the man a license for sex. In my mind, that was a true statement. The woman was supposed to submit to her husband. A large part of the submitting was in the bedroom. I would not always have a choice. In retrospect, it was more of a reflection of his control issues. My past gave me NO rules concerning boundaries around appropriate behavior concerning sex and/or psychologically suitable relationships.

My spouse had anger issues. He also disliked authority figures even though he held an authority position. The ole "what's good for the goose" doesn't apply to the abuser. Basically, I was to do as I was told. For a long time, I did just that. I didn't want to anger him because of my childhood fear of my dad and his angry outbursts. I would do anything to keep the peace. Occasionally, I would stand up to him. I would always regret doing so. I hated the fights. I eventually hated him.

After three years of marriage, my son was born. I was completely mortified. I was a kid myself. He was so amazing and beautiful. The only problem was he didn't sleep for 18 months. I was a physical zombie. Now, I not only had this façade of a marriage; I had brought another human being into this psycho maze. I couldn't see just how miserable I was at the time, but I had to get up and show up for my son.

When my son was 6 months old, I was in a horrific car accident. I was in a car with my friend and a drunk driver hit us head-on at 80 miles per hour. It should have killed us both, but it didn't. At the hospital, my husband was crying saying it was his fault. God was punishing him as he had been having sexual fantasies about the lady down the street. What is wrong with this statement? First, I was the one in the accident—not him. Second, God wouldn't punish me for his actions. There were so many of these crazy episodes in my relationship that I lost count.

We moved a lot because he couldn't keep a job because of his authority issues. I became so depressed and begged God for a sign.

There was never a "sign" given to me. It was the most horrible period of my life. Living with my dad was mentally exhausting; but, living with this man was even worse. My fears escalated, and the stress began to affect me physically. In this trap, the mouse was me and the mouse wanted a way out. There were so many times I wanted to die. I couldn't leave my son with this man. My child was the one person on the face of the earth that needed me. I would never be like my mother and desert him. I realize now my son was a gift that gave me purpose.

It wasn't until I had my daughter and a nervous breakdown that I came to my senses. I became close to someone who was also married to a control freak. We ended up having an affair. I truly loved this man, but we decided for the sake of our children not to pursue it. This was just another example of my pain, suffering, and loss. I felt complete and utter abandonment. However, seeing what the future could be like and that I could escape my hell, I left my husband. The affair gave me the courage to step out of the abuse and try to make a better life for my children and me. I will be forever grateful because it was the wake-up call I needed.

I went back to the only place I had to go…home to my mom and dad. I was 24 years old, had two children and was flat broke. There was no support system back home. My dad didn't want us there, and my grandmother had passed away. I moved into her old house next door. I had two years of college, but no skills. I had to find a job. I went to work for a lighting company assembling light fixtures. I stood all day and made minimum wage. I was so grateful to be bringing in some money. My new life, although hard, was beginning.

My friends and church family looked at me as a "sinner." I even had one church member tell me that I owed the church an apology for leaving my "godly" husband and having an affair. I never apologized. However, the pressure of reuniting with my husband was overwhelming, and I went back to him.

Never go back to an abusive relationship. Statistically that is when most spouses are murdered. Such was the case with me. I went back mostly out of fear, the desire to care for my children, and guilt. He could never get over my leaving him. His control issues spiraled out of control. The whole situation was unbearable. I had loaded guns pointed at me demanding me to stay in the marriage. I had guns pointed at me threatening to kill me. If he couldn't have me, no one would have me. One night he started choking me. It is only by grace he didn't kill me. For some reason, perhaps divine intervention, he stopped. I was already losing consciousness. As I was beginning to fade, I remember thinking, "*Who is going to take care of my kids when I am dead? Am I really going to die today?*" He just sat down and didn't say anything. I just lay there, scared to move and scared not to move. I made up my mind I was leaving— and this time for good.

So, I did. I escaped one day while he was gone. I moved back home and resumed my life with all the people who had judged me a sinner before. This time was different. I still had guilt, but I wasn't going to die in that guilt. I never really shared anything that happened to me. I just seemed to choke it down and tried to make a better life for my children. I started back to college to finish my degree and try to make something out of my life. I began to put emphasis on my own self-improvement. Still, I struggled with depression and anxiety. These were very dark days. The only thing that got me up each day was my kids. The divorce was especially hard on my son. He was old enough to know his dad and had the same confusion all kids face when their parents' divorce. I just didn't have the skills to help him because I was battling my own demons. If I had not had my children, suicide would have been the option for me.

I dated my high school friend. We eventually married. I knew I was making another mistake. My children and I needed help, and he so desperately wanted to help. I had no self-confidence and needed to make enough money to support my kids. With his help, we could make a good life. Our marriage didn't work either. I was a ship lost at sea.

Then phase two of my life crises happened—my daughter developed an eating disorder. It tore at the very fabric of everything I had experienced. From 6th grade until she was a sophomore in college, she battled this disease. I felt I had failed at everything—including protecting my daughter from her own demons. I started to believe that I was meant to fail. It broke my heart that my beautiful daughter was suffering so badly. We all had been through so much, and I couldn't protect her.

I was drawn to self-improvement books, tapes, and CDs. I started a library that is still one of my prized possessions. I got my degree, started a career in banking, and decided to climb the corporate ladder. Through my career, I've met some of the most amazing people in the world, and I've had many new chances to learn. I am remarried to a wonderful man. I continue to learn everyday about relationships and the importance of family in our lives.

The day came that I had to put the proverbial "stake in the ground." Yes, I have a great career. Yes, I set some goals for my life. And yes, I met them. But this precious gift of my life…the good, bad, and everything in between…needs to be shared. I need to tell my story. I need to use my passion and drive to help others, like me, who feel they have no hope. It is never, ever too late to change your life. It is never too late to realize you are worthy of an amazing life.

My story, with its disappointments and adversity, is a reminder of the light of hope that shines every day. We may not always notice, but the evidence is there—the smile of someone when we are having a bad day, the book that somehow gets placed in our path, the kind encouragement you get from someone you barely know, the grace of God that appears often times out of nowhere. Hope helps you find courage when you feel you can't go another step. Hope helps you endure heartache that completely tears your heart apart. This is my journey and it may be similar to your journey. I can confidently say there has been "amazing grace," and the "amazing grace" started with my intention to chart a different course—to walk in a different direction.

I call this turnaround in my life "Being Intentional" and finally determining to be free. It took all the strength I had to go from fear-ridden to fearless. I am resilient, but I am much more IN-TENTIONAL. I decided I was going to change my life and be free, and that is exactly what I did. In finding the strength to do what is good for you (not what is good for everyone else), you find your freedom. When I realized that I endured adversity to be a beacon of hope for others…it changed my life. When I gave up being a "victim" and started living as a "victor," my life changed. You will never find out who you really are if you are living in blame and shame. With forgiveness, you can begin again. I promise you—you can. If I can do it—you can too. You just need to be intentional in giving up the hurt to find happiness, giving up the fear to be fearless, giving up the silence to walk in your strength.

I didn't do it alone. The Universe has given me so many blessings. My greatest blessing is my immediate family and an extraordinary group of like-minded friends who really care and support me in my growth. These friends are my very own "Tribe." Having this type of support is essential for your own growth. Hanging with the folks who negatively judge your actions will only keep you a prisoner to your limiting beliefs. We are programmed as humans to think negatively. It is only by sheer will that we escape the damaging effects of negativity in our lives.

This is the reason I named my story "Permission to be Free." I had to give up blaming my circumstances on others, so I could create an intention for my life. I had to decide what I wanted, and how I wanted to create it. I have always had a yearning to help others to overcome personal obstacles. So, I created a vision for my life down to the smallest detail. I want to use my experiences to help others create a life of fulfillment.

My life vision is this: to use my drive and passion to teach and inspire others how to discover and live the life of their dreams. Here are some of the steps I used to break free:

1. Discover your possibilities. Find your purpose.
2. Create and manifest your dreams—your dreams—not the

dreams someone else has for you.

3. Overcome fear and limiting beliefs.
4. Look yourself in the mirror and love the person looking back at you.
5. Do not live in the "what if life hadn't been this way" mode. You can't erase the past. You can create a new future.
6. Control your thoughts. Don't allow negativity to rule in your mind.
7. Practice daily gratitude.
8. Do a few things every day that result in moving you closer to your dreams.

My life today is simply amazing. If I can start over, so can you. I am just an ordinary person. Stepping out of your mental prison and giving yourself "permission" to have a better life makes you extraordinary. To be intentional means to take the bad experiences of your life and channel them into something positive. You are unique and everything about you is a special creation. When we reframe our hurt and pain and desire to know our true purpose, the possibilities are endless. With a changed mindset, we can accomplish extraordinary things. The starting point to all change is desire—to think differently and to feel differently. There is no "to-do" list when you start. The only requirement is to start. If you can do that, the rest will come.

There is a universal love that surrounds this planet. You are loved. You are worthy to have an amazing "intentional" life. Just know there is hope in the darkness and multiplied peace awaits you. Grant yourself permission to BE FREE.

CHERYL HOWELL

Have you ever asked yourself "What is the meaning of my life? Could I possibly just start over?" We have all asked these questions in moments of despair. Cheryl Howell explores these questions and more and helps others navigate through those moments in their lives when searching for meaning and fulfillment. She always had a "gut instinct" there was more to life…an amazing life to be created. Cheryl takes individuals on her own personal journey of hurt, trauma, abuse, and abandonment. She adapts a very personal method for helping others heal, grow, and succeed. One of her online courses, "Get Angry," is an example of how she weaves the negative emotions and experiences of our lives into a magical healing process.

During Cheryl's corporate banking career, she led high performance teams for some of America's biggest commercial banks. Cheryl Howell is a transformational trainer who inspires individuals and employees to become leaders who continually pursue excellence, direct goals toward personal ambitions, while instilling the principles of maintaining a solid, consistent work ethic.

Cheryl is also a certified trainer of The Canfield Methodology—a proven system of habits, behaviors, and attitudes developed by America's leading success coach, Jack Canfield. After reading The Success Principles—Mr. Canfield's blueprint for top achievers—Cheryl began her journey of living, learning, and loving herself.

Now, Cheryl Howell uses her own expertise to bring others this powerful fusion of corporate and personal experiences to show how pain can become your greatest teacher and your greatest gift. Corporate Banking taught her about building relationships and teamwork while using her own personal experiences to help others grow. Cheryl has a deep-felt soul connection with her clients. She is authentic and honest in presenting the principles that will inspire you to heal, be accountable, and succeed in whatever you choose to do in your life.

Check out her website at www.cherylhowell.com. Explore your purpose for your life with her free question planner on the website. Look at her "Get Angry" course, and follow her on social media.

If you have questions regarding her coaching sessions or courses, email cheryl@cherylhowell.com

Other Contact Info:
FB: @cherylhowell on Facebook
Instagram: @theadversitycoach
Linkedin: www.linkedin.com/in/cheryl-howell-9a389838

PERMISSION EVOLVES AS YOU GROW

LISA NICHOLS

What a delicious and colorful journey it's been . . . giving myself permission to be the "me" I am today. Twenty-six years ago, I was not only broke—I was broken. At the time, being broke was easy—that was just a money thing. Being broke was easier to navigate because I could just find something that I could exchange for value and then accept monetary currency for it.

Being broken, on the other hand, was harder because I had to give myself permission to get back up. I needed to give myself permission to breathe. I needed to give myself permission to turn all of my chaos into my creativity. I needed to give myself permission to be broken and still have possibility in my life.

I had to give myself permission to say, *Damn, you've been in a failed relationship again, yet you're still worthy of love.*

I gave myself permission to get up, you know? Maybe you've been there. You get up. Then life happens and you have to get up again. It seems like you're pressing some reset button. Get up, your mind tells you over and over again. *Get up, get up again.*

And so it was for me in the early 1990's. I gave myself permission to be The Little Engine That Could. It was permission to keep trying, to never give up on my dreams, and when I was so tired I could barely breathe, it was permission to put one more foot in front of the other and keep going.

But, as I evolved, I learned that we all need to give ourselves a different kind of permission: permission to own our brilliance and our worth, but also permission to realize we don't need to show up for anyone else or do what *they think* we should do. We learn that we are the only one writing our autobiography. Each of us is writing our life story, and our life story has to be a bestseller.

It doesn't have to be anyone else's bestseller; it has to be *our* bestseller.

My 90-year-old grandmother often says, "Baby, when you get to be my age, all you're left with is your memories. That's all you have. Your body requires greater focus to follow your commands at 90. Your friends aren't running and jumping to be with you at 90. Matter of fact, most of them are not around anymore. All you're left with is your memories."

Your memories are your life story, so your job is to create a bestseller for yourself—that is, to live a life that you want to be re-read and re-lived and re-shared as many times as possible. You want it to be the kind of life story that will inspire the people you share it with.

By 2010, I was giving myself that kind of permission. After being on The Oprah Winfrey Show, The Larry King Show, The Steve Harvey Show, and countless others, I gave myself permission to be visible in a much bigger way. Permission wasn't any easier then; it was just different. It would still take work and being dedicated to my dreams. I still had to own my worth and command respect. But, the stakes were higher now. The numbers were bigger, and the potential of my impact on the world was bigger, too.

When Steve Harvey asked me to be his personal success coach, I had to give myself even more permission. "Permission granted" looked very different then. I had to give myself permission to charge someone a lot of money to coach them on something that I did effortlessly. I had to give myself permission to have enough belief in my natural skill set to value myself higher and charge Steve what I knew my worth was, but also what I knew he had never been charged before.

There were so many more layers of permission that came up for me in those days, too. Like the time when Dr. Phil invited me to his house to discuss a project, and seated in his backyard listening to him talk for hours, I gave myself permission to set aside the stardust of the moment and wonder, *Where are we going with this? What does this man want?* I gave myself permission to not be so outcome-driven, but to go with the flow. I gave myself permission to lean into it and partner with him—doing five shows—before I gave myself permission to end it all, saying, "I know how popular you are, but I don't really want to play like you play."

Here's the big take-away that I learned by giving myself permission to play with the big boys on my own terms and demand my value: once I could speak up, show up, and stand up for myself, I served the world from my overflow. I wasn't going through some sacrificial martyr experience. I wasn't saying to myself, *I'm going to wait and get mine in heaven.* It wasn't the kind of experience where I begged people to love me, see me, and acknowledge me. It was me saying, *Hold on a moment, who am I? Who do I know myself to be? What are my contributions? How do I show up in this season of my life?*

And, by the way, your season of contribution changes. I had to continue giving myself permission to go through the changing seasons. I gave myself permission to ask, *What does this season look like for me?*

The beautiful (but also utterly devastating) thing I've found about women is that most women have lived a life of selflessness. That means that we become so selfless that we sometimes forget about "self." But, selflessness starts with self. Selflessness also includes self-care. So, when I talk about standing up, speaking up, and showing up, the first person you need to step up for is yourself. When you do that, you become an example to the world of how they should treat you—and how they should love you. When you treat yourself well, you also show others how they get to treat themselves. You become the best role model possible.

Here's an example: I just got back from Dubai. I was actually there twice in three weeks, and I vastly underestimated the level of personal security that I would need when I was there. Not because it's a dangerous place, but because they had rolled out the red carpet for me. I was a crazy-big celebrity before I even arrived. I didn't expect the side of the convention center to have my face on it. I didn't expect His Excellency to request a meeting with me. I didn't get into the human-potential training field for accolades like that. But, they became a byproduct, you know? The "royal treatment" was a byproduct of me standing up for Lisa, speaking up for Lisa, and showing up for Lisa. Then, once I felt full, I could serve the world from my overflow.

Ladies, that's the nugget here. Don't miss it. Don't miss the diamond that I just put out there: *being treated well is a byproduct of you standing up, speaking up, and showing up for yourself.*

Lavishing myself with care and consideration sounds selfish, but here's what I had to learn: self-care is not selfish. Self-care ten years ago was just me being responsible to my future. Too often we say to ourselves, *I'll get mine later. Oh, don't worry about me, I'll be fine.* How many of us have said that? Don't worry about me, I'll be fine. We master that conversation, right? But doing that repeatedly *now* will show itself *ten years from now* as being frustrated and feeling undervalued.

In my own life, for example, I could have waited until my son was 18 before going out and living my dream and traveling the world. Instead, I asked myself, *What if I worked a little harder and did it now while he's seven years old? What if that just means that I need to create a 13-page Jelani Care Guide?* I drove everybody crazy because in his care guide, I knew Jelani's current exams that were due, and the science project that he was working on. I knew what cereal he thought was the most amazing cereal at that moment and the Pokemon Cards that he was fascinated with. I knew everything, and I put it all in a journal . . . a catalog. I gave it to his teacher, my grandmother, Jelani's grandfather, to the childcare worker, and to the neighbor. I gave it to his cousins so everyone would know exactly how to care for Jelani as if I were there in person.

Then, I figured out how to do both: give Jelani his dream life, while I create mine.

I never lived an either-or kind of life. Either-or is scarcity-based thinking. Instead, I've lived "both-and." That's a much more abundant mentality. It's why I wrote the book *Abundance Now*, because I realized I'd been living this "both-and" conversation unconsciously. I didn't talk about it or write about it—I just lived it, both "be a mom" and "live my dream." Once I created my first bestselling book, *No Matter What*, I did media interviews to promote it and got the same question over and over again: "How did you do it?"

I started recalling and retracing what I did. And "what I did" was I made both things work. I didn't subscribe to the common thinking that I could either be a mother or an entrepreneur . . . or that I could be a celebrity or a faith-based speaker . . . or that I could be wealthy or godly.

No. I made the decision to do it all. I realized I can be godly and wealthy. I can be a great mom and a great CEO. I can travel the world and have an amazing relationship with my son. Just get him a passport, right?

I became a woman of action and accountability. I discovered that the distance between you and everything you really want is action and accountability. Unfortunately, most people mistake due diligence, planning, and "thinking about it" for being in action. Hello!? Thinking about it, studying, researching, writing plans in our journal—*that's not being in action.* That's being in thought. They might be some really cool thoughts, but they mean nothing until you apply some real action to them.

I suggest you ask yourself, *Which three steps can I take action on for the next 30 days that will move the needle in a very small way toward getting me to my bigger vision?* And if you keep moving the needle after 30 days, where might you be in 18 months? What are the action steps you can take—and *by when* will you take them? Action steps without a deadline are simply wishful thinking.

Whenever I'm experiencing overwhelm or frustration, it's because I've looked at the details and the process, and I've realized how long it will take and how much it will take out of me. I get overwhelmed and frustrated because I haven't looked at the outcome often enough. I don't focus on why I'm doing it. When I coach myself, I ask, *What are you doing this for? Who is this going to help? Why would you sign up for this?* These questions get me immediately reattached to my "why." When I'm in overwhelm it simply means that I'm stuck in the process. I've become detached from my "why." I'm focused on the 59,000 things I need to do, instead of focusing on the bigger question I started with: *whose life is going to be transformed on the other side of this?*

When I get down and need to pick myself back up, I think about the people whose lives (and children's lives) might be touched, inspired, and transformed because I got myself out of bed. Because I got myself unstuck. Because I got out of my moment of discomfort and despair and got back into my legacy.

And that's the real lesson here, isn't it? You're not writing your life story; you're writing your legacy. Your life is finite. Your legacy could serve my son's children and my son's unborn children. That's who I need you to work for. I need you to get up today for the children of tomorrow. That's legacy.

So, give yourself permission to have all of your dysfunctions, all of your hesitations, all of your labels—yet still be a phenomenal contribution to this planet in a unique way. Give yourself permission to find your unique fingerprint. Not someone else's . . . *yours*. What's the song that only you can sing?

Don't try to sing the tune you sang 20 years ago. Your voice has changed. Your lyrical tones have changed. Why chase history and try to regain your old life when your future is begging for your attention? *I want my old life back*, we sometimes say. *I want that relationship to be like it used to be.*

In closing, remember that you inspire those who are witnessing your life. They're inspired by the way you breathe, but they're also inspired by the way you catch your breath. They're inspired by the way you serve. They're also inspired by the way you stop and say, *I need to rest.* The people you inspire by your hustle and your service are also inspired by the way you sit still and ask for direction and clarity. It's not just your voice that's powerful—your silence and your stillness are equally powerful.

You're more influential than you can ever imagine.

And in writing your own life story—in creating your legacy—with every page you turn, you can read what's next. You don't have to know the entire path; you just need to know the next step. So, I want to invite you to live in your duality: be brilliant and gain clarity. Be powerful, but also surrender. Be a leader, but be an editor, too—deleting those parts of your life story that don't serve you. And as you do all these things in your life, I'll be your sister and friend on the journey cheering you and applauding you.

LISA NICHOLS is one of the world's most-requested motivational speakers, as well as a media personality and corporate CEO whose global platform has reached nearly 80 million people. From a struggling single mom on public assistance to a millionaire entrepreneur, Lisa's courage and determination has inspired fans worldwide and helped countless audiences breakthrough to discover their own untapped talents and infinite potential.

As Founder and Chief Executive Officer of Motivating the Masses, Inc., Lisa has developed workshops and programs that have transformed the lives of countless men and women and altered the trajectory of businesses throughout the country and across the world.

Lisa is also a best-selling author of six books, and her seventh book ABUNDANCE NOW, was published in 2016 by HarperCollins. In ABUNDANCE NOW, Lisa continues her journey with her fans, providing a clear and practical blueprint for personal success, drawn directly from the life experiences of its beloved author. ABUNDANCE NOW is the follow-up to Lisa's New York Times Bestseller, NO MATTER WHAT.

Lisa's extraordinary story of transforming her own life from public assistance for her family to leading a multi-million dollar enterprise is the inspiration behind her bold mission to teach others that it is possible to do the same. Today, fans worldwide revere

Lisa for her mastery of teaching people how to accomplish unfathomable goals and tap their limitless potential.

A noted media personality who has appeared on Oprah, The Today Show, The Dr. Phil Show, The Steve Harvey Show, and Extra—just to name a few, Lisa is also celebrated for the impact she has on the lives of teens. Through Lisa's non-profit foundation Motivating the Teen Spirit, she has touched the lives of over 270,000 teens, prevented over 3,800 teen suicides, supported 2,500 dropouts in returning to school, and has helped thousands reunite with families.

Among the prestigious awards and honors bestowed upon Lisa for her extensive work are the Humanitarian Award from the country of South Africa, The Ambassador Award, and the LEGO Foundation's Heart of Learning Award. The City of Henderson, Nevada named November 20th as Motivating the Teen Spirit Day; the City of San Diego named April 25th Motivating the Masses Day; and the City of Houston, Texas named May 9th as Lisa Nichols Day for her dedication to service, philanthropy and healing.

Lisa lives, plays, and works in the greater San Diego, California area and on stages around the world, working alongside her world-class team committed to Motivating the Masses.

"You playing small doesn't serve the world. There's nothing enlightening about shrinking so others won't feel insecure around you. As you let your own light shine, you indirectly give others permission to do the same."

MARIANNE WILLIAMSON

PERMISSION TO GET MESSY

JEWELL SIEBERT

I pulled into my driveway, took a deep breath, and started to cry. As I sat there, silent tears rolling down my cheeks, I wondered, "What's wrong with me? Why aren't I happier?" I had every reason to be. I had wonderful friends and family, a successful career in the Army working with some amazing people, was married to a man I loved, and had money to travel and take classes. What was my problem? Why was I feeling so drained? So, blah?

My entire adult life, ever since my years as a cadet at the United States Military Academy, I'd had a plan: graduate, become a platoon leader, company commander, primary staff officer, battalion commander…retire from active duty. Things were going exactly to that plan. Still, something was missing.

That "something" gradually wore on me. And over the years, I'd gotten to the point where every morning my alarm would go off, I would sigh, and the first thing out of my mouth was a not-so-polite f-word.

Nevertheless, I stuck to the plan. I'd made a choice and put in a lot of work, after all. The thought of starting over at that point, when so much of my life was good, seemed insane.

Then, everything changed.

My friend and I were walking to our apartments on a beautiful spring day in Seoul, South Korea. I was a major in the Army and a few months pregnant.

The Friday prior, my husband learned that he was one of the thousands of majors being separated from the Army as part of the congressionally mandated military downsizing. As my friend and I walked down the street, she asked how I was doing. Without thinking, I said, "I wish I had gotten selected instead of him."

I was surprised to hear myself say that. I wanted to be a battalion commander. I wanted to retire after serving 20 years.

And yet...

In that morning stillness, with only a few cars on the road and the birds singing in the ginkgo trees, I thought for a long moment.

I realized I had a choice.

"I could get out too."

As soon as the words left my mouth, I felt an incredible lightness that I hadn't felt in years.

Even though being on active duty in the Army had been an incredible gift, it wasn't the perfect fit for me. I felt a pull to do something else and fighting that pull was making me feel drained and unhappy, despite all the goodness in my life.

That feeling of lightness wasn't enough. I still wasn't sure.

The Army had been my life for 17 years since I'd first hugged my mom goodbye at West Point. My choices, my identity, everything revolved around this plan I'd created.

The idea of changing my identity seemed daunting because I was so out of touch with who I was and what I truly wanted. I had many accomplishments in my life, but still there was always a part of me that said I wasn't enough. That I wasn't worthy. That my choices didn't matter. And when we have those types of feelings, choosing to change the status quo brings an additional layer of obstacles.

Those next few months, I didn't sleep much (and not just from trying to find a comfortable resting position with my ever-growing belly). I was afraid to make a choice, and the not-knowing was consuming me.

Then, one day, in one single moment, I knew.

It was the moment my daughter was born. The nurse handed me that tiny pink perfect little baby, and as I held her to my chest—*I knew*.

I realized just how precious our time here is, and how I spend it matters.

I realized that this little girl was going to look to me to be her example. And, if I wanted to teach her to embrace who she truly is and what she wants, I would have to do it for myself. Settling for being happy-*ish* was no longer enough.

I realized it was time to make a change.

Seven days later, my family and I bundled up against the snow, drove to my office, and I turned in my resignation packet.

I felt excited...and nauseous.

Granted, I knew in my heart it was the right choice for me. But, that didn't stop the doubts, the second-guessing, the panic attacks...the feeling of not knowing where I belong or that I might be screwing up my entire life. Was I being selfish?

The path wasn't easy either. Six months after I turned in my paperwork, I left active duty (I'm now in the Reserves) and still had no idea what I was going to do.

It's not easy to start over from scratch. It's scary. It's messy. There's no roadmap. I was literally turning in my boots for binkies, and I can't even tell you the number of times I sat on the bed asking myself if I was making the dumbest mistake of my life. "I mean, seriously, both my husband and I are about to be out of work...with a baby...and no plan. What the hell am I thinking? What kind of irresponsible person does this?"

It always came back to the same thing. Even though I didn't know what I wanted, I knew what I didn't want. And that, at least, is a start.

So, start I did—over and over and over.

I could say that I've failed many times. I tried setting up an online kitchen gadget store that had exactly one customer (my mom bought a cookie cutter). I tried making money with ads on blogs and pocketed a whopping $23. I did freelance work writing vision statements for dentists and doing administrative tasks for friends. Shoot, I even spent two months working as a door-to-door salesperson in the middle of a Texas summer.

I was embarrassed. And, I was afraid of what people would think. Here I'd given up an established career, and I was failing at every single thing I tried. Let's be honest, it's not like I was trying to do something complicated like solve the human genome project. I felt very small… and incredibly foolish.

Yet, I don't count any of those things as "final" failures. As long as we keep trying, failure isn't really *failure*. It's just an experiment to help you see what's next.

Mine led me closer to figuring out what I did want, and—get this—actually made me more confident in myself in the end.

Crazy, right?

Although failing felt just about as good as eating a pine cone sandwich, I saw that no matter how many times I fell down, I could handle it.

I learned that confidence comes from knowing where you're going, paired with taking action. Even though I wasn't where I thought I'd be at this point in my life, I was happier than I had been when I was trying to force myself into a place that didn't fit.

And that's a pretty great feeling.

So, even in the midst of my stumbling, self-doubt, and bruised pride, that sense of lightness remained. I kept trying things out and with the help of my mentors and some serious self-development work, I finally got clear on who I am, what I want, and how to get there.

Easy? Not exactly.

Worth it? Hell YES!

Why? Because, while making a new choice with our direction in life isn't easy, easy isn't the point.

The point is to honor your soul.

The point is to honor the Truth of who you are and what you

want. The point is to create a life of purpose, meaning and joy using the gifts and desires that God gave you.

Giving ourselves permission to make the choices that honor our souls takes us out of our comfort zones. It forces us to re-learn who we are, and to reinvent our realities. Not easy. But always, ALWAYS worth it.

As in, "now-I-wake-up-happy-instead-of-cursing-out-the-alarm-clock" worth it.

What did I learn along the way?

I realized that I had to get really clear.

For example, have you ever found yourself staring into the fridge trying to figure out what to eat? I have. You know you want something, but not sure what'll hit the spot. So, you stand there with the door open, letting all the cold air out, with your mind bouncing from pickles, to turkey, to that half-empty frosting container.

That, my friend, is what it's like when you're trying to decide what to do and haven't figured out exactly who you are or what you want. It wastes energy, and you typically end up with something that's less than satisfying.

When I figured out ME—my values, my wants, my dreams, my desires, what makes me tick—then I could finally determine what was missing. This awareness allowed me the freedom to choose and was the beginning of my path in the right direction.

Another thing I learned was to anticipate obstacles.

In a perfect scenario, once I gave myself permission to make major changes, everything would fall into place, birds would sing, rainbows would light up my path, and life would be easy breezy.

Yeah…That was *not* my experience.

Some days the challenges felt so big that I'd find myself staring at the mirror, asking how I got myself into this mess, and how on earth was I going to dig myself out.

Encountering internal and external obstacles when we step outside our comfort zones is completely normal. Creating a new reality is disruptive in nature. And disruption can quickly lead to discouragement and stagnation if we let ourselves get sucked in.

It's possible to completely reframe the disruption. I realized that by accepting (and dare I say, welcoming) the obstacles as part of the natural process, they were much easier to manage.

I changed my story. I told myself, "It's just another puzzle. I buy puzzle books all the time. These are just bigger…and in 3D." Instead of beating myself up for not being far enough along, I reminded myself that nothing's ever easy at the start. And, I began celebrating the fact that I was gutsy enough to even try.

Each obstacle can also be an opportunity. An opportunity to learn something new. An opportunity to course correct. An opportunity to show yourself that you're so much more than you ever realized.

Once I started anticipating and reframing the obstacles, I found ways to navigate out of the abyss of worry and doubt. I did (and still do) little practices that don't require much time or effort, but that kept me calm and able to focus better. Different people have different techniques, but I can say without a doubt that there's something that will work for you in a matter of minutes, hours or days.

Finally, I learned to focus forward.

I know from experience, second-guessing and self-doubt are a waste of time and energy.

Not only that, but there's an opportunity cost too.

Every moment I spent focusing on what could have been was a moment when I wasn't available for the bigger and better opportunities. I was closing myself off to the good things out there for me because I was so focused on what I might be missing—what could have been.

Once you give yourself permission to make a new choice, commit. Go all in. Fears and resistance will come. It's our subconscious' way of protecting us. The status quo might not be the best thing for us, but it's safe. And, it's a habit that can be hard to break.

When I gave myself permission to make a radical choice, going from a totally set life plan to having no idea what was next, my inner voice amped up the volume. It said, "Maybe I should just stay. This isn't so bad; I can wait it out."

Yes, we can decide that the change is just too much. We can stay where we are. We can wait.

But, and I say this as someone who spent a lot of time waiting it out, when you're in the position where you know that you're settling for less than what you want and what you're worth, then waiting is a disservice to yourself, your skills, and the precious gift of time that you've been given.

Thankfully for me, there was another voice inside that I chose not to ignore.

In my heart, I know that we are all put here on this planet with a special purpose and that we are equipped with the gifts and desires needed to fulfill that purpose. So today, I invite you to take a look at where your heart is settling and give yourself permission to make a different choice: to let go of what might have been, and to create a life that makes you happy to get out of bed in the morning.

Even if you've chosen something different until this point.

Even if you don't know what the end will look like. Even if it feels like it is too late.

And, even if (or rather, when) things get messy along the way.

Permission to choose is yours, and if you stay the path, the path will turn into a journey of a lifetime.

JEWELL SIEBERT

Jewell Siebert is a bestselling author and certified professional coach helping working women to become the best versions of themselves, so they have more fun, meaning and impact in their lives. She helps children to be confident, resilient and kind, so they grow into successful, happy adults who make our world better.

Jewell's mission is to help people to find their "happy" through rediscovering who they are, connecting with what they truly want, and building the confidence to step outside their comfort zones to make their dreams their realities.

Jewell is a graduate of the United States Military Academy at West Point, and has been featured on Bravo, A&E, and in the Huffington Post. She combines her 18+ years of experience as an Army Officer with practical coaching strategies and energy clearing techniques to help her clients achieve powerful transformations in all areas of their lives.

You can find her at:
jewell@jewellsiebert.com
www.jewellsiebert.com
https://facebook.com/jewellsiebertcoach/

PERMISSION TO LET GO

MAGGIE SULLIVAN

> " *No one saves us but ourselves. No one can and no one may. We ourselves must walk the path.*" - Buddha

The journey to awakening can be a long and winding road with many detours and roadblocks put up along the way, but it is so worth it when walking on the right path. Life just seems to work effortlessly and amazing miracles manifest. However, for some, like myself, it requires a tremendous amount of work in the form of personal development, working on mindset, digging deep into my soul, and learning to trust the universe.

Along the way, there may be rough roads or wrong mountains climbed; but with continual perseverance and awareness, when a roadblock shows up, it is easier to recognize the message and trust to choose another path or stay the course. All is not lost when reflecting on the many lessons that were presented along the way. Lessons can be in the form of people, places, and events. I believe the universe has inserted these events along the path so that better decisions can be made. It took me a long time to learn to trust the universe, over fifty years actually–but then, when I did, my life changed.

My long and winding journey started at an early age. My dad died from a heart attack when he was 42. I was three years old. My mom suffered from mental health issues and used alcohol to ease her pain. My siblings were much older than me, so I felt like an only child. A lonely child. I spent a lot of time with myself.

I understand that my mother did the best she could and through doing work on myself, I have learned how to release the anger and resentment I felt for so many years. I was angry she was unable to parent me in a loving way. I felt she kept me playing small for many years by teaching me to believe that dreams do not come true. My mother had this habit of always saying that planning was a waste of time because if things do not go according to plans it leads to disappointment, so don't bother. She would say this because my mother and father had planned on going on a trip before he died. Her plans with him never came true. That belief kept my mother stuck, and I adopted it as well.

I loved my mother, but we were not always loving towards each other. As a result of her mental illness, we fought often which ended with me acquiescing to her demands. I developed a pattern of searching for her approval and trying to please her. That coping strategy drove me for far too long. It continued into adulthood, and I became a people pleaser filled with self-doubt, always over-achieving to compensate for my limiting beliefs. I poured myself into my studies, my work, my family, committees, and people pleasing activities. Saying no was never an option for me. I constantly lived with my limiting belief that I was not enough and needed to be, do, and have more.

It was not until I was in my mid-forties that I received my first whisper from the universe. It was from a friend who had passed away. It was delivered to me through a medium. The medium told me that my friend wanted me to do something with the flowers. I didn't understand the message, but being a reflective person, I concluded that she was trying to tell me that I needed to give myself permission to stop and smell the roses and learn how to love and take care of myself and do less. My schedule was so full I never allowed time to just be present and enjoy what was in front of me.

I honestly didn't even know where to start, and this is where my journey began. I started by reading self-development books written by great thought leaders. I listened to podcasts, master classes, and attended many personal development events, so I could wake up a little more each day. My self-confidence and self-esteem grew, and the little voice in my head that told me I wasn't good enough was beginning to fade away.

I started becoming more present in my life and doing more things that did not involve working all of the time which was so foreign to me because I was a teacher. As a teacher, I was here to serve others, but this time, I decided to put myself first. I went on trips and spent more time taking care of me. But self-doubt can be like a bad weed, if you do not remove all of it, it comes back even stronger. The weed is like that little voice in your head that shows up and challenges you, *Are you sure you are ready?*

My dormant self-doubt did indeed return with a vengeance soon after my mother passed away. I realized there were some unresolved childhood issues that I still needed to address. I went to work with a therapist, did additional reading, journaling, meditating, and seminars to deepen my self-love and self-worth. I really thought I was close to eliminating the self-doubt and limiting belief, but it resurfaced in full force, stirred up by an event that shook me for a couple of years.

After working at the same school for 21 years, I was involuntarily transferred to a different school. I was not told the specific reason why I was being transferred, only that changes needed to be made in the organization, and I was the change. I felt betrayed and rejected which resulted in reawakening my dormant limiting belief of not being good enough. It was as though my childhood trauma was colliding with my adult self. "What the heck," I thought, "will this ever go away?" I had done so much work on myself and my self-esteem. I was devastated and found myself facing my old issues again.

When I had to say goodbye to my colleagues of over 20 years, my heart suffered. My spirit was broken. I reached a whole new level of self-doubt in my life. These people had been my tribe, and I was theirs. Now, I was on the outside. I felt sad, small, isolated, which resulted in a depth of doubt I hadn't experienced until now. And it wasn't an overnight experience—it lasted over two years. At times, it diminished when I was surrounded with the right people. But, it would sprout like that weed when I was triggered.

I was tired of this, and it led me to take a workshop where I had this aha moment—you know those defining moments we all have, the ones that could potentially redirect your future—well this was one of those. The name of the workshop was Renewing your Spirit. I left that workshop realizing that I am the creator of my life and no one else was going to determine my future. I am the one who is responsible to create the best life possible.

I continued doing personal development work and came to the realization that I needed to make additional changes in my life. I did the scariest thing I had probably ever done—I left my full-time employment to become an entrepreneur and start a business of my own. It was still very difficult to completely release my on-going feeling of self-doubt, and it continued to reappear. There were many times I wanted to quit, but I didn't because of this little voice. It was the voice that would eventually take over, but it had been driving me all along. I was finally starting to become aware of its message. I began embracing the voice that would go on to support this new version of me.

I had to come to grips with the knowledge that transformation, like everything else, is a slow process. I persevered. I continued with my routine of rising early and journaling, meditating, and reading. I continued digging for answers and solutions to my issue of self-doubt. I also continued to surround myself with uplifting people. As well, I sought conventional therapy and alternative therapies such as Energy Healers, and RIM Facilitators (Regenerating Images in Memory). I believe that all of this supported my healing journey.

I continued doing all of this until one day I made a decision. I surrendered. I gave up all blaming, complaining, and excuse making. I realized that all of these situations were presented to me so that I would grow as a human and become the best version of myself. I consciously stepped into the new me.

I began to fully recognize that I am worthy, and that I am a gift. That old belief that I was not good enough, which clouded my judgment of myself, was a story that no longer served me. It was not true. I no longer allowed other people's opinions to derail me. I realized that since I created that belief, I could just as easily create a new belief, so I did. This is an example of choosing my responses with intention and choice rather than reacting to them.

It is always a choice. We can choose to think negative or positive thoughts, so we might as well choose positive thoughts. My new belief is that I am a gift to this world. It is said that our chance of being born is one trillion to one. If I can be the answer to even just one person's prayers, then I have made a difference in this world.

Once I accepted this knowledge of my uniqueness, I vowed to never let anyone else create my reality. If I am the creator of my life, I deserve to make it a great one.

Today, I see my transfer from one school to another was a gift from the universe. It allowed me to finally wake up and realize my uniqueness. I was more than a teacher to just one classroom at a time, I was destined to reach a vast number of people to help others overcome self-doubt and believe in themselves. The unwanted transfer got me out of the classroom. Had I stayed in that comfortable place, I wouldn't be where I am today. I am living proof that if you give yourself permission to let go of what no longer serves you, then you can have the life you deserve and were truly meant to live.

I have a new purpose. I speak from my heart so that I can help others experience inner peace and self-awareness. I share the stories that stayed with me for so long so that others can avoid that same trap that kept me stuck.

I admit it took me a long time to wake up to the belief that I was a gift. But when I did, I woke up even stronger. Surrendering gave me an incredible feeling of power. I was able to fill up a hole that was buried deep in my soul. I have been released, and now I am completely free. I'm creating my life on my terms. I feel lighter, happier, and more inspired to help others free themselves from whatever may seem like a limit to them. Every time, I speak up and encourage others to reflect on the patterns in life and to confront areas that are not serving them, encouraging them to give themselves permission to let go–I become stronger as well.

Here are five practices that have worked well for me. I encourage you to ponder:

1: I start my day with an hour devoted to me.

I devote an hour to myself each morning to check in and reflect. This keeps me on course and grounded, never allowing those limiting beliefs to take me off course. I write in my journal, meditate, and read something positive. I reflect on situations where I have chosen to give up blaming, complaining, and excuse making. I celebrate myself for who I've become in the process.

2: I continue to look for patterns in behavior that could keep me stuck.

If I keep doing the same things and keep getting the same results, I have learned that I need to choose a different response. I check in with any fears or limiting beliefs that may be getting in the way of me living to the fullest. I know now that self-doubt can disguise itself as perfectionism or protection.

3: I practice self-love every day.

I say no to others, so that I can say yes to me. I am gentle with myself. I give myself permission to use adversity as a learning opportunity put in place by the universe. The life lessons help me grow and become my best. I practice a growth mindset to keep me from playing small and this growth mindset gives rise to choosing better responses which leads to better outcomes.

I have built a "Self-love Container" and have filled it with tools that remind me to give myself permission to love myself. In my tool box, I have written down the names of the people that I can call when I need a boost, the places that I can go that will bring me joy (time in the sun), and the things in life that remind me of my inner beauty (thank you cards from friends and clients).

I celebrate my wins by writing them in my journal. I fill my body with healthy foods and plenty of water. I continue to get rid of stuff. I take a few moments to let go of old papers, notes, clothes, and unnecessary memorabilia to help create space for love.

4: I surround myself with positive people

I surround myself with people who lift me up. I prefer to collaborate with people and not compete because together we can help each other. And when I am faced with challenges, I am brave to have the difficult conversations necessary to move forward. I believe that in order to continue to grow and build capacity institutions, organizations and individuals ought to engage in difficult conversations.

5: I believe in myself and I trust the universe

I always remember that I am a gift. I do not take things personally. I am open to the miracles that the universe delivers to me daily. When I believe in myself my self-esteem rises and I am confident. I live by the words of Eleanor Roosevelt, "No one can make you feel inferior without your consent." I give myself permission to let go of words that do not serve me so that I can rise to be the best person that I can be. If my story is no longer serving me, I write a new story with a better ending.

I would like to end with a word of caution—transformation may be a long process and is easier said than done. I have learned to give myself permission to take the time necessary to become the best version of me. It took me many years and many reminders to choose happier, more positive thoughts over deep dark thoughts. It took me constant daily work on my mindset to overcome bouts of low self-esteem. My daily work allowed me to release limiting beliefs. It has brought me to where I am today—living a life of joy and inner peace.

I believe it is important to become the most awakened person that I can be. I continue to grow in my self-awareness daily. I fully enjoy this journey, and I am patient with myself. I am now aware of the synchronicities that happen in my life.

Life is too short to only stop and smell the roses, I need to be the gardener of the roses and take the time necessary so that I bloom to my full potential. I am so happy and grateful that I am finally on the right path. I would love to be of service and share additional tools to help others find the best possible path to awakening. You can reach me at maggiesullivan.ca.

MAGGIE SULLIVAN

Maggie Sullivan is committed to helping awaken people to reach their highest potential. Born and raised in Ottawa, Ontario, Canada, she attended Carleton University and completed her Bachelor and Master of Arts in Sociology. She received her Bachelor of Education at Nipissing University in North Bay, Ontario, Canada and worked as an elementary teacher for over twenty years.

Maggie took an early retirement to fulfill her true passion—helping others deepen their self-awareness and inner peace. Maggie inspires people through sharing her stories of adversity and perseverance in keynote speeches, and live events. Her online courses focus on topics of everyday life, and they outline how to create and enjoy a beautiful life.

Maggie Sullivan is a #1 Best Selling Author, Certified Canfield Methodology Trainer, Speaker, and she has recently published her first children's book, The Story of Max.

Maggie is married and has two sons, Alex and Andrew. She currently resides in Northern Ontario, Canada and loves to travel to warmer climates.

To book Maggie for speaking or training:
Email: msullivan@persona.ca
Website: maggieSullivan.ca
FB personal page: www.facebook.com/maggie.sullivan.180
FB business page: @fromtheheartwithmaggiesullivan
www.instagram@maggiesullivanfromtheheart
www.twitter@maggiefromheart

"*Once you begin to understand and truly master your thoughts and feelings, that's when you see how you create your own reality. That's where your freedom is, that's where all your power is.*"

MARCI SHIMOFF

PERMISSION TO BE ME

DONNA NUDEL BROWN

A few years ago, I was preparing for my 35th high school reunion and was eagerly awaiting and excited to answer the questions, "So, what's going on?" "What's new?" "What have you been up to?" I had finally accomplished something significant since I graduated high school and for the first time, I felt proud of where I was with my life! I still kept in touch with a handful of friends whom I held close to my heart. Apart from that small group, I was unlikely to see my fellow classmates unless by a chance meeting while home visiting family.

The evening of the reunion, I arrived early feeling proud and excited to share my news as I walked into the party room. The first people I saw were two of my closest guy friends that I had seen only a smattering of times over the years.

"So, what's new?" they asked.

I could barely contain myself. "I am about to become a published author!" I said.

"Really, what did you write?" they asked.

"My story." I said.

"What is it about?" they asked.

"My journey." I responded.

"I don't know what that means," they said. "What story?"

"Well, the story of my life, and how I got from where I was to where I am now." I answered.

"AND????" they said, puzzled.

I said, "I realized my belief that I was not smart because I left college before graduating kept me playing small for many years." I paused and noticed they were both standing mouths agape.

"What?" I asked.

"You thought you weren't smart?" they responded, surprised.

"Yes," I said awkwardly.

"You should have called us. We would have saved you 30 years of anguish."

I must have looked puzzled.

"You were one of the smartest people we knew in high school!" They said emphatically.

"What?" My heart jumped and sank simultaneously. "*How could that be*?" I thought.

"You don't remember your good grades?" They asked, "You don't remember how well you did?"

"Well sort of," I said, "but I failed classes in college, and I never finished."

"That doesn't prove anything," they said, "Did you try?"

"Honestly, not 100%." I responded with embarrassment.

Don't you think that is why you didn't finish and that it had nothing to do with you not being smart????" They asked with sincerity.

Wow, wow, wow! In that moment, I indeed wished I had called them years ago.

We all have a journey. Sometimes, it is easy and predictable, but life is also filled with challenges, which can lead to self-doubt and feelings of unworthiness. If you are open to seeing it, the obstacles—highs and lows, unexpected turns, and tough decisions—are just opportunities in disguise. Today, I would not trade my journey even though at times it felt SO uncomfortable, unfulfilling, and miserable!

Two months after my reunion and that conversation, I was excited and nervous to be standing on stage in Philadelphia, along with my brave co-authors, as we launched "Women Who Ignite"—the collaborative book that included MY chapter. As I shared my story *"Finding Fabulous at 52"* with the crowd that evening, I had a revelation. Thirty-three years earlier, I had left that same city feeling like a failure. That night, I felt like a huge success. I was a published author!!! It was one of those full circle moments I will never forget. That moment happened because I had finally said yes! "Yes" to myself. "Yes" to living out loud. "Yes" to facing my fears and showing up anyway. I said "YES" to leaping off a cliff which gave me the courage to follow my intuition and led me to say "Yes" to owning my gifts as a coach, Reiki Master, author, speaker, and trainer. "Yes" to facilitating workshops incorporating the healing power of crystals, and I even said "Yes" to performing as a stand-up comedian!

None of these things would have happened if I hadn't taken the risk, faced my fears and emerged with more confidence and courage than ever before. Taking that risk helped me understand the power and necessity of working on myself at a whole new level.

My journey of self-development began in 2008. I was catching up with a friend who shared she had done a series of workshops that allowed her to look at events differently—as merely events with no stories or meaning attached to them. That's when I decided I needed a way to see things differently as well. At the time I recall not feeling happy or fulfilled, and I remember thinking there had to be more to life than where I was—a stay at home mom caring for my family. Know that I love my family dearly, but I remember often introducing myself as my children's mother and not by my name. I had lost my identity and wondered what my purpose was beyond being a mom. My children were growing up fast and would soon be on their own. I was desperate for an identity of my own. Once I began my journey of self-discovery, exploring who I was and who I wanted to become, I began to see shifts in how I looked at life and my place in it.

As I reflected on my past, I realized I never really felt like I fit in. I have a memory of starting middle school and noticing most of the girls wearing Jordache jeans. I didn't have them, and I never would because my parents wouldn't buy them for me. It made me feel less than, unworthy, and as though I didn't belong. I think that is when my self-talk started, and I am sure it wasn't kind. I would ask myself, *What was wrong with me? Why was I always on the outside looking in?* I wanted so badly to be in that tight circle with the girls in their Jordache jeans and not on the periphery. Would wearing Jordache jeans have put me in the circle? I'm not sure they would have. My response to not having what others had or looking like everyone else was to dress so differently there would be no chance of comparison. I had a style all my own, and a senior class superlative to prove it.

High school was a whole new level of not fitting in with friend groups, boys, and parties. If I were invited, I often couldn't relate. Other times, I wasn't invited at all. Again, I experienced feelings of loneliness and isolation, of being outside the circle. I wanted to be included so badly, and when I was not, I ultimately realized I needed to seek friendships outside of those circles.

The interesting thing is, I knew when situations, relationships, or places didn't suit me or feel quite right, so I would intuitively remove myself even though I desperately wanted to be included. I have always had a strong intuition and knew when my circumstances didn't feel right to me, I just couldn't articulate it or identify it at such a young age. Since I always had those inklings, I assumed everyone had them. I later learned that those qualities were gifts that allowed me to tap into my inner guidance. While I understand my talents now, back then, I only felt the pain and loss of not belonging.

I had never been part of a large group, but over time, I began to sense where I fit in and was accepted. I have always preferred one-to-one relationships and thankfully, through the years, I have had close friends who have supported and loved me, a confidant for every season. I have a timeline of friends, and I treasure each of them and all that they have brought to my life. I can't imagine my life without them.

In 2014, I met a group of women and truly felt like I had found my tribe. You know those friends who support you and accept you for exactly who you are, regardless of what you do for a living, how much money you have, or even what kind of jeans you wear—they love you unconditionally. These women lift me up, cheer me on, encourage me, listen when I need a supportive ear, and applaud me when I have victories no matter how small. They have become my biggest cheerleaders.

In this tribe, I have found my place where I truly belong. There is something so profound in knowing that I fit in. This sense of belonging has filled a void in my heart and soul that I hadn't realized was there until I took a step back and realized what had been missing most of my life. That profound sadness from a loss of connection was no longer there. I am happiest and most content when I surround myself with others who are in alignment with who I am, and who support my beliefs and how I show up in the world.

I will admit that occasionally I still suffer from FOMO (Fear Of Missing Out), and I recently learned of a new acronym FOLO (Fear Of being Left Out). Knowing that I am not alone and that others have dealt with these isolating feelings is comforting. I used to think I was the only one who felt that way. Even now, when feelings of 'less than' emerge, I chant the mantra I learned years ago— *"I am smart, I am beautiful, I am worthy, and I am enough."* When those feelings of doubt creep in, I simply remind myself of these powerful words, and I choose to believe in myself.

I recently attended a workshop where we identified our core values and explored how they influence our everyday lives. I had already known that humor, trust, and respect were important to me. I was excited to learn what else would be revealed.

We were asked to create a timeline of our life, listing each memorable event in chronological order, and then assign a value to each memory. Positive events went on the top half of the page and negative events on the bottom half of the page. My results were astounding! I assigned the value of belonging to 90% of the events that were below the line, since they *lacked* belonging. With the exception of becoming a mother to my three children and other significant life events, the majority of the positive events I experienced were within the last 10 years. I was astonished at the outcome, but it was as if all the pieces were finally falling into place. Once I learned the power of positive thinking, mindfulness, the Law of Attraction, and having an abundance mindset, I was able to reframe and view every event with a different lens. I had changed my awareness and learned to look for the positive in every situation. I could see positives in events I once viewed negatively. With this new awareness and knowing my core value of belonging, I was able to attract like-minded women, create new collaborations, and new opportunities to share my gifts and talents.

I was so focused on not fitting in; I didn't realize that my inner voice and dialogue were creating my reality. Simply by changing my thoughts I could change my experiences—attracting everything and everyone I wanted in my life. I had it in me all along, just like Dorothy and her red slippers. We have so much power over our lives; I can't imagine how my life would have looked if I knew this as a teenager.

It wasn't until someone who'd read my story shared that they identified with me and wanted to connect with me that I knew I had found my purpose—supporting women in finding their voice, pursuing *their* true purpose, and seeking a life of joy. I needed to share my stories and my gifts with other women. It was time for me to embrace my inner teacher and my wise self. I pinch myself most days when I see how far I have come. I became masterful at hiding my true feelings and beliefs about my life. My outward persona did not match my internal sense of lack. When I share my story with others, it is often met with surprise and accolades for who I have become. I recognize that the perception we have of ourselves can be so vastly different from the perception that others have of us. I know the difference for me was enormous!

I am extremely proud and grateful for that day, not so long ago that I said YES to leaping off that cliff! That leap literally gave me my voice and allowed me to embrace the path I was meant to live. It has enabled me to impact the lives of others and I am proud of the many lives I have touched.

Every decision, every thought, and every belief I had created the tapestry of my life. I believe my compassion was built from my struggles, my intuition from my needing to find my way, my empathy from the pain I endured as an outsider looking in, my tenacity from the need to figure it out and survive, and my humor from needing to ease my discomfort from my feelings of lack. All the times I felt out of place and alone, it was often humor that got me through. We all have obstacles and we all have gifts—finding our way to use those gifts to overcome our obstacles is the greatest gift we have. I believe I have truly mastered that skill.

Today, when my coaching clients have those 'AHA' moments,

or my Reiki clients instantly feel the healing power of energy, I am filled with gratitude. When my clients receive their crystals in the mail and share that they feel the energy from them even before they open the envelope, I am so filled with joy. I want the world to experience the magic I feel.

I want you to know that you have the power to change from where you are right now. If you are not happy or fulfilled, and you feel as though you are not living in your purpose, you can take action to find your joy. We all have the power to change—to follow our head, our heart, and our gut to get us from where we are to where we want to be. Remember, the *how* is not up to us! We all have that ability—first we must trust, then we must believe that we can, and then we must take inspired action to create change. We all deserve to live a life of joy, to live in our purpose, and to make every moment count. Do not ever allow anyone else to squash your dreams or determine your worth.

I learned long ago that what other people think of me is none of my business. I so wish I could tell my 13-year-old self that not having Jordache jeans didn't matter, "*Continue to be exactly as you are— you are uniquely you, and you are a gift to the world. Do not change or compromise for anyone or anything unless it is your heart's desire. Be you, always be you.*" I have memories of going into the store, trying on the Jordache jeans and staring in the mirror knowing I couldn't have them. There was some solace knowing they didn't even look good! As I recall this memory, I am literally laughing out loud! To me the crime at that time was that I couldn't have them; I think the bigger crime is that if I could have them, they would have looked horrible!

To this day, I still am hesitant and will not buy something just because 'everyone else has it'. I am ME and that needs to be reflected in how I show up, physically, emotionally, artistically, materialistically, spiritually, and most importantly as authentically me.

At some point I unknowingly decided I would not compromise who I was in order to fit in or be included. The few times I allowed myself to bend the rules 'just that once', I regretted it and experienced a sense of betrayal. Shortly thereafter, I decided that if it wasn't a "hell yes!" for me, then it was a "no"! Even if Jordache jeans made a resurgence, I still wouldn't buy them as an homage to my 13-year-old self. I didn't need them to be amazing then and certainly don't need them to be amazing now. She and I have exactly what we need to be smart, resilient, caring, incredibly strong, compassionate, and freaking fabulous just as we are!

It has taken a long time, but I can say with certainty, I am proud of who I am! I am proud of how I show up, and how I have learned to support others using my unique viewpoint and gifts that I have mastered. I have finally given myself Permission to Be ME—exactly as I am!

I look at my incredibly talented, intelligent children and am grateful they each know their own gifts and strengths. I am watching them soar and stand in their power as young adults, and I can see how filled with confidence they are. As a mom who felt like I needed an identity of my own, instead of being identified as my children's mother, my proudest accomplishments are those three amazing souls I have raised. Now that I have found my identity, know my purpose, and the reason I am here, I am ecstatic when I am introduced as my children's mom!

If you feel as though you do not belong or fit in, I encourage you to seek out people who share your interests and passions. There are so many avenues to meet people now—

join a group, take a class, or do something you have always dreamed of doing. When you are living in your purpose and meeting others who share your passions or interests, you will find your tribe. Keep looking, they are out there! We all deserve to feel as though we belong...

I am Smart, I am beautiful I am worthy, I am Enough!

Crystals to Clarity • with Donna Brown
Donna@DonnaBrownDesigns.com • www.DonnaBrownDesigns.com

DONNA NUDEL BROWN

Donna incorporates all her Lightworker gifts as a Reiki Master, Crystal Healer, Coach, Author, Trainer, Speaker, and your *personal* Cheerleader. She guides her clients step-by-step in uncovering their true passions and desires, including sharing techniques to confi-dently make decisions in all areas of their lives. These techniques rely on energetic responses whether using a tool such as a pendu-lum or simply your body's response through muscle testing. Ener-getically, your body knows what it needs before you know intellec-tually.

Protecting yourself energetically is crucial and Donna provides practical tools and techniques and offers solutions to raise your vibration and clear yourself of negative energy that does not serve you. She is passionate about crystals and as an Energy Intuitive se-lects the exact right ones for her clients to best support them. She is grateful for her ability to guide clients through her Crystal Chakra Balancing and Reiki sessions since energetically being in alignment is crucial and can easily be achieved from a distance.

Donna became a #1 best-selling author for the second time re-cently with the release of the collaborative book "Women Who Rise". She was previously a co-author in "Women Who Ignite" published in 2016.

Donna created her *Finding Joy Video Series* to share many of the techniques she used to find her joy: https://www.donnabrownde-signs.com/finding-joy-video-series

To learn more about her Chakra Balancing sessions, please visit: https://www.donnabrowndesigns.com/product-page/virtual-crystal-chakra-balancing

Donna sends Reiki to her clients around the world; to learn more, please visit her website or reach out to her at Donna@donnabrowndesigns.com

She is here to support you! One of her core values is providing a sense of belonging and Donna wants you to feel that you belong and are welcome in her community; she is always available to connect.

Contact info:

Donna@DonnaBrownDesigns.com

www.donnabrowndesigns.com

Instagram: @crystals_to_clarity

FB: @donnabrowndesigns

LinkedIn: https://www.linkedin.com/in/donnabrowndesigns/

PERMISSION TO BE ONE WITH MY CREATIVE SPIRIT

JENNIFER GRANGER

I see you,
I am you
and I offer you these words
to guide you to your knowing.

It happens
every
single
time.

When I begin to create, I can feel a deep connection to a knowing presence within me. I feel a flow from a source so pure and full of truth. It's my creative spirit that surrounds me in silence and also intense inspiration. I am most me in this flow; it is all I know.

I know, even as I type these words that appear on the page before you, that every single word will have a very specific purpose. And, that purpose is forged from my creative spirit as I surrender and simply allow it to shine through me, shining through my love for all creation.

As I am in the midst of my creations, whether it be hours, days or months, I know that each of my creative moments is connected and fully on purpose. I feel centered and aligned to the impact I know each will have on the lives of others. I may never know all the ways my creations influence the world, but I do know that if I stay connected to my love for creativity, they will always be of the highest service.

Each creation is crafted with my love for creating space so others can use this space to discover a way to be fully present in each moment. I am grateful for my connection to spirit, so much so, that I want to help others achieve this same connection. When you connect to spirit, living each moment with intention provides clarity. It's like the clear sounds of a wind chime when the breeze blows. The notes drift into the air and are effortlessly carried to the ears who find delight and joy. Connecting to spirit can be just like this once you are aware of what lights your soul on fire.

This is the connection that is infinitely bonded to your human journey because you reach a deep awareness about who you are and how you are meant to show up for all the other souls in this world. It's as if you've always known this feeling through all time or maybe infinite time.

I also know that I am a spiritual being on a human journey. So, when there are times that I feel lost or completely off course in the messiness of living, I usually experience a major challenge that literally stops me in my tracks. And then it happens—I hear the loud cry from my warrior soul, and it screams, "Remember me, come find me again through your mediation and in the sacred space your journal pages."

That moment is when I know it will be okay.

I know I can survive the mess.

My practice of meditation and journaling opens the connection to my soul, to my creative spirit. During these days or months, my creative spirit craves curiosity and wonder because they are the light source that leads me through the darkness of my fears. My practice is always about finding the light within because that light shines brightest through my creations.

And then it happens, I connect back to spirit

every

single

time.

I wish that each of you reading these words know this same journey with your soul. Honor your journey because this is the space where you can expand the light you shine in the world. Be humble. This is our time to be fully present with our awareness of why our souls came into being. Take care to see your inner light and use each moment to shine and be present with that light. Explore what spiritual practices or rituals enhance the connection. Find the very quiet space where you can simply connect to your soul.

It's a peaceful moment when you feel this grounding influence at your core. You know you are showing up truly as you and your gifts are so rooted in exactly what is meant to be shared or created in this time and space. This is your journey to shine.

It's when you get to this space that you simply know,
every
single
time.
I honor you with this poem, so you can always know
every
single
time.

The Knowing from Your Soul
By Jennifer Granger

The moment you soar with your soul space, you know.
The moment you take flight without effort, you know.
The instant that you become one with your soul space,
you know deeper than any other knowing.

Fly sister, fly
Fly sister, fly
You are at peace gliding in the thin veil of your soul space.

The moment, the wind takes you away, you know.
The moment, you breathe with the flow, you know.
The second you become one with the light,
you know this is for eternity.

Shine sister, shine
Shine sister, shine
You are called to live in the brilliance of your infinite light source.

The moment the world expects you to fall back, you know.
The moment the pulling of your just fine life calls you back,
you know.
The time you scale the peak beyond your dreams,
you know there's no return to mediocrity.

Rise sister, rise
Rise sister, rise
You now get to live in the knowing with your soul.

The moment, the soul space expands beyond any boundaries,
you know.
The moment, the universe loves you infinitely, you know.
The 'right now' becomes unbound from the constraints of time
and you simply surrender.

Fly sister, fly
Fly sister, fly
The universe welcomes your soul to a journey of
infinite possibilities.

JENNIFER GRANGER

Jen Granger is a #1 Best-selling author, Speaker, and Creative Living Mentor.

"I believe everyone is creative. Every action we take creates the journey on the stepping stones of our life. When we understand this creative power, we can harness it for a lifetime of being aligned to our soul's truth on the journey."

Over my lifetime, I can clearly connect the dots in all the ways my life was created by me. It didn't just happen to me. I actively participated in creating the life I was living (the good and the not-so-good parts).

Today, I am more mindful as a create my life. I rely on what I call "creative living" practices or rituals like meditation, crystals, moonbeam energy, intentional journaling, visualization, and expressing gratitude. When I am mindful, I support my journey to create the life of my dreams.

Through my daily practice, I discovered that my passion is to share my creative living knowledge with others. It is my deepest joy to fully step into my role as a creative living mentor with individuals, groups and corporations or organizations. I help people see that they can create the space in their own life for a journey of infinite possibilities.

Follow me on my blog and receive updates on my creations and programs at www.mysunrisesisters.com or email me at jen@jeng-creations.com.

PERMISSION TO SURRENDER

JANET ATTWOOD

Have you ever let go of it all? The most remarkable things can happen when you surrender completely. Letting go and trusting in the universe is probably the all-time greatest challenge anyone can face. Walking in the dark with total blind faith, not knowing where the next safe footing will be, afraid that the unknown will unveil more than we can take.

One of my first experiences of consciously giving myself permission to hand it all over to the universe was in 1980. I was in a job recruiting disk drive engineers in Silicon Valley and was failing miserably. Luckily for me, one day after work when I was meditating in the local meditation center, I opened my eyes and glanced upon a sign on the bulletin board that advertised a success seminar called "Yes To Success" to be held in San Francisco the following weekend. All circuits firing, I knew that somehow the answer to my prayers had everything to do with taking that seminar.

My intuition couldn't have been more on! Not only did I take the seminar, but I eventually persuaded the seminar leader, a vivacious and passionate woman named Debra Poneman, to hire me. As luck would have it, Debra was going on her U.S. speaking tour at the same time I was to arrive in Los Angeles, where her company was located, and she needed someone to house sit. She said I could stay in her apartment, study her success tapes while she was gone, and when she returned, I could start my illustrious career, uplifting and speaking to hundreds of people all over the world.

I was in seventh heaven!

Two weeks later, after Debra and I finalized our plans, I said goodbye to all of my friends at the recruiting firm, packed my bags, filled my vintage red Toyota up with gas and headed down to Los Angeles, radio blaring, singing at the top of my lungs, ecstatic that I was on my way to start my dream career.

Two miles into my journey my little red Toyota started sputtering and spurting. Steam started rising up over the front of my car from inside the hood and as I was pulling over to the side of the freeway to see what was going on, my trusty little red car took one big breath, let out the most God awful sound and died.

Horrified, I just sat there frozen by the side of the freeway, stunned at what had just happened.

After the initial shock of losing my beloved Toyota, I came up with an alternate plan to take a train down to Los Angeles. After paying to have my car towed, buying my train ticket to Los Angeles, and then taking a long taxi ride to Debra's apartment in Santa

Monica, to my dismay and alarm, I arrived at Debra's door with $13.00 to my name.

Afraid that Debra wouldn't hire me to go out and teach other people her success principles if she knew I was completely broke, I said nothing while we were together and kept a sunny smile on my face until Debra finally waved good-bye to me.

"Now what am I going to do?" I thought to myself. Feeling totally weighed down by the fact that I hardly had enough money to last me more than a few days, I went to Debra's refrigerator and scooped myself a huge serving of her chocolate ice cream. After eating almost the whole half-gallon, I laid down on her couch and fell into a drunken chocolate sleep.

When I awoke, I decided there was only one option when things got this bad.

I grabbed the keys to Debra's blue Chevy which she had said I could borrow for emergencies and headed down the Coast Highway with a renewed sense of hope. I knew my poverty state would soon be over.

Arriving at the great Saint Paramahansa Yogananda's "Self Realization Fellowship Meditation Center" in Pacific Palisades, I immediately felt a deep sense of calm take over me. I walked past all of the beautiful buildings to the majestic and serene gardens that graced this special place.

Reaching into my purse, I pulled out my treasured, crisp one dollar bills and stuffed all $13.00 into a little wooden donation box that was located in the garden.

When I had donated all I had, I sat down on a nearby wooden bench and had a very intimate talk with God, pouring out my heart and telling him all that was going on with me and where I could use a little of his support.

After a little while, I walked back to Debra's car, knowing that letting go of all the money I had left in the world absolutely had to be the best thing I could have ever done. I didn't know why I felt that way, but I did.

I headed back to Debra's apartment, and the minute I walked in, the phone rang.

"Hello," I said.

"Janet, is that you?"

"Uh huh. Who's this?" I asked.

"It's me, Patrick."

Patrick was my ex-husband's father, whom I totally loved, and hadn't heard from in over a year.

"Hi Patrick, it's so nice to hear from you, how did you find me?" I asked.

After we chatted on the phone for some time, he invited me to meet him for lunch at a nearby restaurant.

Patrick was unbelievably animated and talking 100 miles a minute. He had just started selling a natural weight loss program he was really excited about. He put four bottles of the stuff on the table and said this was just the beginning for me.

"Janet," he said. "I think this is something you could really make a lot of money on in your spare time if you wanted to."

Patrick still had that same sparkle in his eyes I had always loved. When he spoke about the products he had set down before me, I couldn't help but start to feel excited about it too.

"The opportunity sounds great," I said. "How about when I

have some extra money, I'll order some from you?"

"I don't think you should wait that long," Patrick said to me smiling.

"I just happen to have $500.00 worth of the stuff in the trunk of my car. You can have these bottles on the table and the $500.00 worth as well. Pay me back after you sell it and make some money for yourself."

Just as he handed over the four bottles our very overweight waitress walked up to our table and said to me, "What's that?"

I told her everything I could remember that Patrick had just told me about the products.

"I'll take everything you have!" She immediately whipped out a $100.00 bill from her apron, grabbed the bottles, and walked away.

I sat there stunned and overjoyed. Thanking Patrick as we said goodbye, I headed home.

This experience was a profound lesson for me. One which I've remembered often during the twenty-six years since these events took place.

We are always taken care of. Giving myself permission to trust and donating my last $13.00 was my way of surrendering to that force which is always looking after us. I learned that all that's required of me is to let go of my agenda and surrender to God's will.

When we do that, the result is always better than what we could have come up with on our own. From that day forward, I never looked back and trusted that each time I came to a new fork in the road I just needed to remind myself that if it worked then, it will work now.

I went on to speak to millions of people around the world and eventually wrote my book *The Passion Test* with my partner Chris Attwood. The book went on to be a New York Times Best-Seller, and with that, my life is better than anything I could have imagined. I had no idea that my last thirteen dollars would be one of the most defining decisions I would ever make.

We all have those moments. I am so grateful I was open and able to follow my intuition and take the actions necessary to become all that I am today.

JANET BRAY ATTWOOD

Janet Bray Attwood is the co-author of the New York Times Bestseller, "*The Passion Test-The Effortless Path to Discovering Your Life Purpose*," and "*Your Hidden Riches – Unleashing the Power of Ritual to Create a Life of Meaning and Purpose.*" She is also co-author of "*From Sad to Glad: 7 Steps to Facing Change with Love and Power.*"

As an expert on what it takes to live a passionate life, she has presented her programs as a featured speaker to hundreds of thousands of people around the world including, The Dalai Lama, Sir Richard Branson, T. Harv Eker, Jack Canfield, Lisa Nichols, Stephen Covey, Brendon Burchard and others.

Janet has taken hundreds of thousands of people through The Passion Test process all over the world. She is the co-founder of The Passion Test Certification Program, which has over 3000+ Certified Facilitators in over 65 countries. Janet is also the co-founder of The Passion Test for Business, The Passion Test for Kids & Teens, Enlightened Bestseller program, The Passion Test Reclaim Your Power Program for the homeless, and The Mastery of Self Love Program.

Janet co-founded one of the first online magazines, "Healthy Wealthy n Wise." Prior to becoming a top transformational leader, Janet worked in the corporate world. In one of her positions, she was the marketing director for the 3rd largest book buyer in the United States, "Books Are Fun," managing the marketing department of for over 40 marketers. It was during her tenure there that the company was purchased by Readers Digest for 360 million dollars.

Janet is a facilitator of "The Work of Byron Katie." She is also a facilitator of the environmental symposium, "Awakening the Dreamer – Changing the Dream" and a "Certified Strategic Synchronicity Leader."

Janet is a founding member of the Transformational Leadership Council that Jack Canfield, the co-author of the "Chicken Soup for the Soul" series, created after taking Janet's Passion Test.

For her ongoing work with the homeless and kids in lockdown detention centers, Janet received the highest award for service from the President of the United States, "The President's Volunteer Service Award." Janet received the "World Peace Flame Award" from the Life Foundation International for her work in promoting peace.

In 2013, Janet was knighted by The Order of the Orthodox Knights of St. John in Recognition of her commitment to the Healing of Humanity. In 2016, Janet received The Transformational Leadership Council award for her excellence in leadership.

Janet presently lives in Europe and travels the globe. For 27 years she lived in Fairfield, Iowa, (your favorite vacation spot!) a community of over 3,000 meditators from around the world.

Janet has been a practitioner and teacher of the Transcendental Meditation Program for over 45 years. (That makes Janet around 47 years old!)

"If you're facing what looks like a large problem, receive it as a compliment from the Universe. What a great soul you must be!"

MARY MORRISSEY

PERMISSION TO TRUST
MY INNER VOICE

TONYA LISENBY HENDLEY

Do you remember what it felt like to wake up the morning of your birthday when you were a child? The anticipation, the excitement, the delight! On June 1, 1984, I woke up with that feeling. It was my 10th birthday.

Even though I didn't expect an all-out celebration, birthdays in my home usually created a lightness in the normally heavy atmosphere. I bounced out of bed, dressed for school, made myself cereal, and waited to be acknowledged for what I thought would be my special day. I thought wrong. My mom was helping my younger brother and sister get ready for school. No one even mentioned my birthday.

Feeling quite alone and a bit sad, I headed off to school. I decided on the bus ride I would not tell anyone it was my birthday. The chance that no one would make it a big deal was just too much to bear. I wondered if anyone would know or care.

At school, I was surprised when one teacher wished me a happy birthday. I thanked her, but there were no more surprises. At just 10 years old, I was already accustomed to feeling forgotten.

After school, I walked to softball practice. I was not a great student, but softball was where I excelled and where I felt the least invisible. I had a great practice, worked hard, and I was starting to feel a bit better about my day. But my spirits sank as I waited for my mom to pick me up after practice. She was usually late; but after waiting an hour, I realized she was not coming. I had no choice but to start the long walk home. I hadn't walked this far in my whole life. What was close to a mile seemed like ten to me. Even worse, I had to cross a four-lane highway which was terrifying.

I felt a pain deep in the center of my chest. My heart hurt. I could not understand how my own family could forget my birthday. When I finally arrived home, all I wanted to do was go to my room and cry and feel safe in my own space. There was no car in the driveway. When I tried to open the door of our very tired, run-down trailer, it was locked. I didn't have a key. I couldn't even go inside my own home.

I breathed in the warm June air and wiped the sweat from my face. I looked around our littered yard for a place to sit and walked over to the large ditch that ran in front of our trailer and the road. I sat with my back leaning against the earth and questioned everything. "How could a mother be so checked out and selfish that she could forget her child's birthday?" "How could she forget to pick her up from practice?" "Shouldn't someone be home to greet a 5th grader after school?" "How could any child…No. How could I possibly be that invisible?"

I sat in that ditch crying, sobbing in a way I hadn't allowed myself to in a long time. At my house you were not really allowed to cry. I'd learned to hide my feelings. I'd learned to go numb. This day was different. I was alone and hurt. I allowed myself to feel all of the emotions I had stuffed down in order to survive.

With tears streaming down my face, I asked God, "Why?" Something clicked. I heard a voice—my voice—clearly in my mind, and it said, "Shut up and get up." The voice told me it was going to be okay, that I was loved, and that everything I needed was already within me. I had no idea what this voice was at the time, I just knew it eased my pain and stopped my tears. I trusted it. In that moment, I remember standing up, dusting myself off, and waiting with a sense of peace for someone to get home; it was almost as if it was happening in slow motion.

When my mom finally arrived, she didn't mention my birthday or that she had forgotten me at softball practice. She was just sorry the door was locked, and it was late. I had this calm feeling that no matter what, I was going to be okay. I could survive, even if it meant going it alone. This was the moment I gave myself permission to trust my inner voice.

I didn't realize what that voice was in that moment. In fact, I didn't realize it until 30 years later when I was talking to a long-time friend about staying positive. We discussed how we create our future, and how so many people fall prey to their circumstances allowing their lives to be dictated by a single incident or a bad childhood. My friend knew about my childhood, the abuse I suffered, and my very fresh divorce. She asked how I overcame such a challenging upbringing to become so positive and successful. I told her I just remember always having a deep knowing within me that everything was going to be okay. That's when I remembered sitting in that ditch and hearing my inner voice for the first time. That voice has helped me rise above my circumstances. It is always there urging me forward. I know for certain I am never alone. I think none of us are really ever alone. We just have to listen and trust and take action when we get those inspired messages.

Does that mean that everything in my life is ideal? Of course not! There have been many days I have had to remember that 10-year-old girl who had the guts to get up and trust that God/ the universe would provide. Listening to my inner voice has given me the courage to go to college with very little encouragement and no financial help, to transfer to a bigger university after freshman year, to leave my teaching position and take a chance at a sales and recruiting job, and to bounce back from losing my career after 13 years on the job.

Strengthened by my inner voice, I took a side step in my career to spend more time with my boys and made a very difficult choice to end a marriage that was not serving any of us. These are just the big ones; but my intuition is real, and I rely on it every day, even for the small things.

My tenth birthday revelation was one stop on a journey I light-heartedly call my crazy, challenging life. I STILL have moments of self- doubt, unworthiness, loneliness, depression, and anxiety. I am quick to give love and support to others, but struggle to let others love and support me. My experiences as a child showed me that it's not IF people will disappoint me, but WHEN, and that people don't follow through. I did not feel I was worth enough for people to honor their promises. I felt all relationships were conditional. Years of reflection taught me that I didn't want to ask for help because I didn't want to set myself up for disappointment. I am taking steps in all my relationships to be more open and vulnerable. Hearing your inner voice does not solve all problems, but it does offer guidance. I have come to trust and listen to that guidance more often than not.

I now recognize the story of my tenth birthday as the catalyst for my soul's journey. A journey filled with poverty, hunger, drugs, physical, mental, and sexual abuse. It's also a journey filled with the opportunity for massive transformation. Sometimes the easy route is the one we already know, the one filled with a lot of pain and resignation. I chose the hard route and truly discovered myself.

In 2015, I was struggling in all aspects of my life and my inner voice had become more of a whisper that I was ignoring because listening would have meant having to take action. Out of the blue I was asked to join a weekend women's retreat. I didn't know any of the participants; I had no idea what the event was about; and, I was so broke that I had no business spending the money to attend. Yet, my inner voice whisper became a yell and would not allow me to give any other answer than "yes." While "yes" seemed ridiculous, I knew my intuition was calling me to once again trust. So, with all my fears and self-doubt, I went for it. I am grateful every day for yet another defining moment in my life—where I chose me. It was the first time in years I had put myself first, and it was the beginning of me living my life with intention and choice. It has been five years since that weekend, and I have grown into who I was born to be. I am in a place in my life I never imagined possible.

My path could have taken such a different turn if I hadn't given myself permission to say "yes" to me. It is something I remind myself of every day. Watching my children learn and grow reminds me to continue to live with passion and follow my purpose. I am grateful for the bad days that bring lessons and the amazing days that bring miracles. I am proud of myself. I am a loving mother. I have three super talented and awesome sons. I am college-educated and a very successful recruiter. My home is warm, loving, safe, and inviting. Our door is always open to anyone in need. It is a home filled with family, friends, and love.

Today, my mission is to empower others to listen to their inner voice. I want to remind others that they are worthy of following their dreams regardless of their story. Our stories are just part of our journey, they are not our destination. I want to help others reflect and forgive themselves and those who have hurt them. Forgiveness is key to redefining one's story. I have an amazing relationship with my mom and my family that would have never been possible without love and forgiveness. This is the amazing life I live now, and it's all because I gave myself permission to trust my inner voice.

TONYA LISENBY HENDLEY

Tonya was born and raised in Cheraw, SC. She's a 1996 graduate of Clemson University and has a degree in education. For the last 20+ years, she's worked as a successful recruiter fueled by a passion for connecting great people and companies. She is raising three very talented boys on her own.

Tonya is also a Jack Canfield Train the Trainer certified trainer. In 2018, she and her best friend, Lori Phillips, created an online community to share their experiences and learned tools with others. They currently run The Positive Vibe Tribe on Facebook sharing daily positivity and support to thousands of members. They have a YouTube channel, Finding Your Way with Lori and Tonya, bringing weekly guidance on how to live a more fulfilled life, and through their business venture, HigherNavigation.com, they are providing webinars, workshops, retreats, and courses on how to navigate to the life you deserve.

The Positive Vibe Tribe:
https://www.facebook.com/groups/206626039828963/
Finding Your Way with Lori and Tonya:
https://youtu.be/RkGsjbpPqw8
Higher Navigation:
www.facebook.com/Higher-Navigation-2097862443839377/
Website:
http://highernavigation.com/

PERMISSION TO TRUST YOUR GUT

LORI CREECH PHILLIPS

3,285 days living a sub-optimal life. There were many moments over this nine-year period of time that were phenomenal. However, during this time, there were not many days that were optimal because even when I was having a good day, the pain and shame were still there.

In 1999, I was a vibrant 25-year-old with my entire future ahead of me. I returned home after spending a fun weekend with friends and my entire world changed. My stomach felt like someone was stabbing me with a dagger and I found blood in my stool—a lot of blood. There really are no words to prepare you for that experience. Your mind tries to make sense of it, but worst-case scenarios run rampant. It turns out that I wasn't literally dying like I thought. However, it was serious. I was diagnosed with ulcerative colitis.

But, let's back up. As a child, I was very discerning, sensitive, observant, and shy. I chose not to speak much, especially to those outside of my immediate family. It's funny to me because most children get fussed at for being too loud or too noisy. That wasn't an issue with me, yet my silence was still a problem for society. I got in trouble for not speaking to people. This was especially frowned upon in the South where manners are a high priority. In second grade, even though I made really good grades and didn't cause any trouble, my teacher wanted to hold me back because I was too shy and didn't speak enough. Looking back now I can see how this led me to trust my instincts a little less and to believe that being me was not good enough. So, even though I was painfully shy, I adapted to what the world needed for me to become so that those around me were comfortable.

You would think this is leading to a sad story, but this adapted version of me had a blessed childhood. I grew up in a family and community that were full of love and support. By the time I left high school and the sweet little Southern town that I call home, I was much more outspoken, but also a little more likely to allow the world to dictate who I was versus tapping into my true self. I found it was just easier this way—don't be too much of anything and hide how you really feel. All of these stories that I told myself and believed to be true contributed to my roller coaster ride with the health care system.

So, here I was in 1999, newly diagnosed with ulcerative colitis, and I quickly became a medical experiment. I had reactions such as spikes in blood pressure, skin rashes, and nausea due to the medication. I spent over a year in an experimental loop—taking a new drug, having severe reactions to it, going back to the doctor, taking a new drug, etc. It was like I was stuck following the directions on a shampoo bottle—wash, rinse, repeat. All of this was on top of the fact that my ulcerative colitis was still active and painful. At the time, I had a long commute to work every day with no restrooms available on my route. I got really good at not eating anything all day and at putting on my game face on the way to work so that no one would know how I felt.

After about a year, my doctor finally found a medication that worked for me with no immediate side effects. I began to feel more like me than I had in a long time. I began to focus more on myself rather than on my disease and opened myself up to new opportunities. Since I was confident that my colitis was under control, I started dating and pursued my master's degree. I was working forty hours a week and attending classes all while maintaining a new relationship. Life was good.

It didn't last. There was a shortage of the one medication that was keeping me in remission, and I went from managing my colitis to going through another trial and error period. My medication mess, the stress of work, school, and a new relationship landed me in the hospital for a week. I had worn my body down to the point of exhaustion and a full-on colitis flare. When I was discharged after five days, the pants I had worn to the hospital barely fit because I had been pumped full of steroids and fluids. I was on high doses of steroids for a long time after my hospital visit and my treatment now consisted of intravenous infusions of medication every other month. I rapidly gained about fifty pounds and began to have even more symptoms that should have been red flags that this was not the right treatment plan for me. Holistic medicine is the health of the whole person—body, mind, and spirit—but my body was breaking down.

The last year of my graduate program is sort of a blur to me. I worked full-time during the day, studied at night, and traveled for my graduate program all while being very sick. My relationship was now long distance because he had moved to pursue his graduate degree. I was so busy with work and school that I didn't see family and friends too much during this time. In my mind, this was for the best because if they didn't see me, then they wouldn't know how badly I was struggling. I hid out in my office to protect my co-workers from my volatile attitude. The medicine had me so agitated that I couldn't trust myself to be kind. My mind was wavering.

The medication caused other problems too—skin irritations, nausea, headaches, more weight gain, and lupus-like symptoms. So, before I turned 30 years old, I had a gastroenterologist, a dermatologist, and a rheumatologist and each of these prescribed their own medications. In addition to the pain of living with active colitis, I had gained 100 pounds and my skin and joints were so inflamed that I could barely walk. I lived in a second-floor apartment at the time. I brought groceries home one day and stood at the bottom of those fourteen steps praying that I could make it to the top. I don't know how long it took me, but let's just say that I am glad I didn't have any food that could have spoiled. This is not how I imagined my life. I was bloated, obese, had skin issues, was severely depressed, hurt all over, and had pulled away from my family and friends. My spirit was broken.

During this time, I distinctly remember putting on my brave face to go see my family—outfitting myself with my armor to hide how I felt. One time I gathered up the courage to go to dinner with a friend who had not seen me in a while. I was so ashamed of how I looked after gaining so much weight and didn't want anyone to see how much pain I was experiencing. I met her in the parking lot of a restaurant and as we walked to the door, I saw there was a step—one step. I panicked and began praying to God to help me get up that step and not let her see the level of my pain. My heart was racing, and I almost had a full-blown anxiety attack in that parking lot over one step. I mentioned this to her recently and cried while I told her—as if I was reliving that moment over again. She had no clue. I had succeeded. Mission accomplished. That was my goal in life during this time—do not let them see how awful it is; that you would rather die than have anyone pity you; how you feel so ashamed and weak and that you have mustered up all of the strength and courage that you possibly can to face them. Looking back, I believe many lessons from my past caused this irrational behavior—the world telling me I was too shy, too quiet, not enough. As a sensitive person you can internalize all of these lessons as truth. So, when you are faced with a struggle, like a life-changing illness, you do what you are told and don't let anyone see how it is slowly killing you.

Through all of this, I was successful in my career; I had family and friends who loved and supported me (when I let them); I had a job that worked around my doctors' appointments and a man who loved me. Instead of feeling blessed, I was depressed. I could not see the good in any of it. I felt guilty that the man I loved was stuck with the sick girl. I felt sorry for myself. I was angry that no one could see what was happening to me even though I deliberately hid my pain. It was like I was sleepwalking. Somewhere in the midst of the medications and the pain, I forgot to connect with God and with my inner self. My body, mind, and spirit were depleted.

A turning point for me was in 2006 when my sister nearly died. During one of the times that it could have been the end of her life, I received a call to get to the hospital immediately. Flying down the interstate to her that day I felt the spirit of God with me. I prayed out loud and cried and shook as I begged for her to be okay and eventually, she was. It was a turning point because although I had no hesitation in asking for God's help for someone I loved, I had forgotten to ask God for help with my situation. I had forgotten that God is always available. I had forgotten that I have a soul within me—God within me. I was so focused on my pain and suffering; I had forgotten that I could tap into the power of God for myself.

In my gut, I knew that I was miserable in my body. The medicine made my brain foggy, and I just didn't want to live my life that way any longer. Everything I had been feeling and hiding and not wanting anyone to see for the past nine years spilled out onto the floor of my doctor's office once I trusted my gut and finally found my voice. He agreed to take me off of all medication. When I had my next visit with him after being on no medication for a period of time, although I was still having issues with my colitis, all of my joint pain was gone—GONE. He looked at me that day and sincerely apologized. I know that it was God within me that replied by forgiving him immediately. I told him I believed I suffered for a reason even though I didn't know the reason. Perhaps it was to provide hope to whoever is reading this story right now.

Stopping the medication didn't solve everything. I was now 100 pounds overweight and in financial debt due to getting a master's degree and from medical bills. I had pushed away all of my friends, and I was not fulfilled at my job. My mind was spinning. How do you think those conversations in my mind went?

Dummy, why didn't you listen to your body earlier and stand up for yourself?

Why did you let the doctors belittle your concerns about weight gain?

You've wasted the best years of your life playing the victim and being weak.

What if your husband stops loving you because he can't handle the depression, the debt, and how you look? He didn't sign up for this.

Your mind does crazy things and it can be a cruel and deceitful place to live. The reality is that many of us live there—in our minds.

For me, it was too difficult to deal with changing my mindset at that time. I started with listening to my body. I am to this day on no prescription medications for my colitis and have been in remission for over ten years. I am hyper aware of my body's signals and honor my body by resting when needed, staying hydrated, and using supplements and food to keep my colon healthy. I have learned to listen to and trust my gut. It is non-negotiable.

By divine intervention, the friend that met me in the parking lot of that restaurant many years before, invited me to a women's retreat in 2015. Although we didn't know exactly what we would take away from this retreat, we promised each other to be open to the possibilities. You see, although I had come out on the other side of sickness, my body, mind, and spirit were still not functioning at optimal levels. I had not processed or released all of the pain, shame, and sadness that I experienced. I did like many people do and just kept pushing it down and moving forward.

I walked into that retreat with my barbed wire safely wrapped around me, so much so that when the other women at the retreat tried to hug me, I declined. I had buried my true self so deeply under a protective shield I put up to spare myself and others that I was offended that they wanted to invade my personal space. I truly was trying to be open, but I was completely defensive. I had gotten so good at closing myself off and retreating into myself because I didn't want to expose my pain. I didn't want anyone to know how miserable I was even though it was written all over my face. I was just trying to make it day to day—going through the motions. I was pretending to be okay even though I wasn't. My world had gotten smaller and smaller because I was hiding myself. I was over-whelmed by my own mind chatter. I was playing the victim story over and over in my mind even though I hated that story. I didn't want anyone to think I was weak or to pity me, but I still told myself these things repeatedly. I remember observing and listening and rehearsing surface-level answers in my mind just in case some-one asked me how I was really feeling.

We rated different areas of our life and for my personal joy I scored two out of ten. I had been promoted at work and was finan-cially doing better than ever. I was married to the man I loved who stood by me during my darkest period. My colitis was in remission, and I was no longer in physical pain, yet my personal joy was a TWO. I should have felt blessed—instead I felt broken, disconnected, and pathetic.

I made a promise to myself and to my friend to be open, so I let the women at that retreat see glimpses of the real me and gradually removed the walls I had built around myself. I am still connected to these women today. I have opened up and have allowed myself to receive their love, support, and advice. My healing journey involves my body, mind, and spirit—and it has been a journey. It is filled with daily practices such as meditating, journaling, reframing negative thoughts, and living intentionally. I continue to participate in mastermind groups, personal development programs and trainings, and accountability partnerships. Instead of being so focused on what others think of me and being so trapped in my own thoughts, I am now more concerned with being a better me today than I was yesterday. I know that gut feeling I have had my entire life—even as a shy, observant, sensitive child—is my inner self, God within me, showing me the way. I am learning to trust this guidance and act on it more and more. As a result, I am living my life with renewed hope and excitement.

I still have moments when I run my body down, and I can feel a colitis flare-up coming, and my default mindset is fear. My mind sometimes takes me straight back to when I was a victim of my disease, and I get angry with myself all over again for not advocating for myself. But, I have grown through my experiences and no longer ignore the early signs of a flare-up and can turn those thoughts around more quickly than ever. My issue was literally in my gut, but this experience with my health has made me acutely aware to trust my gut in all areas of my life. Because of the daily practices, I am now more in tune with my body, mind, and spirit which allows me to be more aware of my inner guidance and to be open to see the things that I used to pretend not to notice.

Too often we don't listen to the signs because denial and settling seems so much more comfortable. But at the end of the day, is it really? It's scary to look at what's real. Sometimes the choices we have to make are so scary that we try not to look at them. Ask yourself, what are you pretending not to know? What is your gut trying to tell you? I invite you to really explore these questions for yourself. If you are waiting for someone to give you permission to take a hard look at the things you are not seeing in your life and to trust your gut to guide you in the right direction, permission granted.

LORI CREECH PHILLIPS

Lori Creech Phillips is a Master Certified Health Education Specialist® and a Certified Canfield Trainer in the Success Principles with over 20 years of experience leading and facilitating teams and training in the government sector. She received her Bachelor of Science degree from Clemson University in Health Science and her Master of Public Health degree in Health Policy and Administration from the University of NC at Chapel Hill.

Lori utilizes the knowledge she has received on creating a positive mindset and living intentionally in her daily life. Because of the growth and improvements that she has experienced in her own life from this work, she has entered into a business partnership with the friend that invited her to the 2015 retreat and they are now creating space for others to learn and grow. This includes a Facebook group, The Positive Vibe Tribe, which brings daily positivity to thousands of members; a YouTube channel, Finding Your Way with Lori and Tonya; and their business, Higher Navigation, at http://highernavigation.com, where workshops, trainings, and retreats are offered.

The Positive Vibe Tribe:
https://www.facebook.com/groups/206626039828963/
Finding Your Way with Lori and Tonya:
https://youtu.be/RkGsjbpPqw8
Higher Navigation:
www.facebook.com/Higher-Navigation-2097862443839377/
LinkedIn: Lori Creech Phillips
https://www.linkedin.com/in/lori-phillips-8989a47/
Website
http://highernavigation.com/

PERMISSION TO GOAL FOR IT

DARLENE WHITEHURST

I remember Easter Sunday, right before the walls caved in. I was the shy, quiet daughter—the one who didn't want to be the center of attention, the one who just loved to dress up. That afternoon, I refused to take off my patent-leather shoes and beautiful yellow Easter dress to go play alone in the sandbox.

My father was in the Navy. We didn't see him much, but I was very close to my Mom. I adored her. Like most women in the 60's, her job was to take care of her family. She was my everything back then.

I was a happy child, full of dreams and aspirations, seeing life through a lens of infinite possibility and on a journey to embrace everything it had to offer. Then suddenly, when I was eight years old, my world turned upside down: my father left us for Mom's best friend. He packed up his new family and left—in the middle of the night, without any means of support, without even saying goodbye.

Not only were we thrust into a world of welfare and uncertainty, we were the only family in the whole school going through a D-I-V-O-R-C-E. Thinking back to those awful days, I remember my first experience with embarrassment: I was standing in the lunch line with my free meal ticket when I heard my name over the intercom to come pick up the school books provided by the county. It was my first memory of wanting to hide, to blend in . . . *to be invisible.*

Eventually, my mother got a job as a waitress, and I had to grow up fast so that I could help her with the house and family. I became responsible at a tender age—a self-appointed "co-mom." I used to walk her to work in the mornings. Then, at night I'd start dinner before walking her home again. We navigated this "new normal" and made the best of things.

But, by the time I became a teenager, I wanted to experience more out of life.

While my friends were at the beach, I was happily cleaning condos so I could earn my own money and feel more independent. I decided to attend college, too—something novel in our family. With the help of student loans and a part-job time, I worked my way through college. In my junior and senior year, I landed an internship in the advertising field. It was my passion and, once I graduated, it became my dream career.

I created something I called "treasure maps" (which we now think of as *vision boards*) covered with my loftiest professional dreams and wishes—then worked enthusiastically to achieve these business goals. As soon as I reached a goal, I tackled new ones. I was always raising the bar.

For me, succeeding was not only gratifying, it was exhilarating!

Then, something quite astonishing happened to me when I was 33 years old. I had an otherworldly experience: a message came to me about work I was being called to do. *Inspire and reach the masses*, the messenger said.

Who me? I thought. *There must be some mistake!*

I was just a print salesperson—a girl on her own, renting a townhouse, trying to decide who to marry. And I was shy. I didn't want the spotlight.

Wouldn't you be better off finding some teacher or speaker who already has the gift of inspiring people? I replied.

And yet, in spite of the fact that I didn't think I was the right person, I responded, "Okay, but I'm not ready yet. I'm going to need some time."

In the next few years, I started my own marketing and branding agency. But I also began a journey of personal and spiritual growth. I dug into new findings in neuroscience—fascinating studies on the power of setting goals and maintaining positive intention. Of course, my own habit of setting goals had completely changed my life and acting with intention was consistently bringing my dreams to fruition.

Why doesn't everyone do this? I wondered. *Why did my mom struggle for so long? Why didn't she teach me this when I was young?*

It's because she simply didn't know. Like most people, she had never learned the power of goal setting and the benefit of being intentional in one's actions.

That was my "a-ha" moment.

It was the answer to my calling years before. I realized I could inspire transformation in people—helping them learn the process of goal setting and right action.

Soon afterward, at a meeting I attended, I witnessed how powerful a group of women can be: as volunteers, in book clubs, running the carpool to school and back. They will come together to support everyone—*everyone except themselves, that is.*

Then it struck me: what if I brought women together and directed their inherent passion and energy to helping *each other* achieve their goals and dreams? What if I created tools and strategies to guide women on a path of personal empowerment?

And that is how the GoalFriends movement was born.

Suddenly, the passion I developed to bring this new style of personal development to the world surpassed that of being an entrepreneur. It became my life's mission. I loved creating the methodology, the branding images and the lexicon to bring GoalFriends to life.

And once it got out into my community, it began to go viral. It caught on like wildfire! The faster it grew organically, the more petrified I became because it required me to be the public face of the new movement. Being a lifelong introvert, I discovered that you can't just magically stop being an introvert. It's hardwired into your brain. Somewhere inside, I was still that humble little girl who never wanted to be in the spotlight.

While I had spent my entire career as an entrepreneur running an award-winning ad agency—carving out a persona and dressing up and owning the space as an expert in my field—suddenly I was way outside my comfort zone. I had "dressed up" my entire adult life, only to now have to begin "undressing" and letting people into my introverted, private world as the leader of a global movement.

Outwardly, my mantra for the GoalFriends movement was, *Clarity equals confidence, and confidence is empowering.*

But my internal mantra became *Public equals terrified!*

I devoured all of the self-help books I could find, but even Brené Brown couldn't deliver enough on vulnerability and courage to help me out. Then I reached out to my friend and mentor, Patty Aubery—Jack Canfield's business partner and the woman who helped create the bestselling *Chicken Soup for the Soul* publishing brand. Stepping in as the Chief Visionary Officer for GoalFriends, Patty insisted that I face the public as the Founder of this magical community that I had built as a labor of love.

And, she said, *I had to own it.*

The first time I took the stage to promote Goalfriends at an event, I may have been surrounded by my peers, but I was riddled with fear and anxiety. Still, I gave myself permission to stand there and be vulnerable so that I could stand up for women everywhere. It was a leap of faith and it required a lot of moxie on my part.

Before that speech, staying small had been comfortable, yet now I decided that I was going to really live! It was the start of my own becoming, to live bravely, to become the person I was called to be. If you want to build the new in you, you must be willing to let go of the old that doesn't serve you anymore.

Today, I'm a perpetual "work in progress," but I'm becoming more and more comfortable as I connect with amazing women around the world and witness their transformation and collaboration as they support each other to achieve their dreams. There are now Goalfriends in the United States and overseas: in universities, non-profits, corporations, and affinity groups. It has become a global brand attracting women of all seasons, who have the desire to work on their goals as they also inspire others who want more out of life.

I hope this is a story worth sharing—one that will inspire you to get outside of your own comfort zone, no matter which barriers may be standing in your way. Remember that you don't have to do it alone. There are women all over the world—like Patty and like me—who are ready to embrace you on your journey and help you make an impact.

Permission is granted. Step into your full potential, achieve your dreams, and move forward to serve the greater good—one imperfect step at a time!

May all your dreams and goals matter.

DARLENE WHITEHURST

Passionate About Your Brand.

Darlene is the President of Adsource Media, Inc/am3 adsource, an award-winning, WBENC certified marketing and branding agency headquartered in Raleigh, North Carolina.

As a female entrepreneur for over 20 years, Darlene and her team have provided creative, innovative and integrated solutions in marketing, media, and brand management to Fortune 500 companies, specializing in healthcare and regulated industries.

Consistently ranked as an expert in her field, she is also a three-time MVP award winner of the coveted *Supplier Diversity Leadership Award* honored by a Fortune 100 corporation. Recognized for her efforts in diversity and inclusion through minority partnerships, her passion to empower others led to her recent company, GF Global, LLC.

Inspiring the World One Goal at a Time.

Darlene is the Founder + CEO of GF Global, LLC featuring the global brand, *GoalFriends*®,

and the Director of the GoalFriends Global Foundation.

She has built and currently leads an international community of over 1,000+ female members. Her programs are designed to inspire life transformations by teaching strategies on dream making, goal setting, and purposeful living. She has made it her life's mission to teach transformational strategies of empowerment through her GoalFriends programs, and to serve marginalized communities through the foundation efforts. She is also passionate to work closely with millennials, thereby cultivating our future female leaders.

She is currently publishing her book, *Goal.os.ophy – You Reap*

What You Goal, available in the fall of 2020. Born in Vallejo, California and raised in Virginia Beach, Virginia, Darlene resides in Raleigh, North Carolina and shares her time in Santa Barbara, California. She is a lifelong learner, thought leader, and world traveler. Darlene enjoys entertaining with family and friends, and of course, her GoalFriends.

"Surround yourself only with people who are going to take you higher."

OPRAH WINFREY

PERMISSION TO DREAM

JENNIFER WRIGHT

I was in my 6th grade classroom when I saw the Space Shuttle Challenger launch on live TV. My class had spent the last few weeks learning about the history of spaceflight and cool facts about the Space Shuttle. We'd learned all about the science experiments planned by Christa McAuliffe, who was chosen to be the first teacher in space.

Three classes of kids were stuffed into my classroom, sitting around a small TV that my teacher had wheeled in on a cart. As we watched the launch countdown, the newscasters talked about how cold it was in Florida. It was even colder in my hometown. The room was buzzing with energy because we couldn't go outside for recess and it was almost lunch time. And then we heard it: "10...9, 8, 7, 6, we have main engine start, 4, 3, 2, 1...and liftoff...liftoff of the 25th Space Shuttle mission, and it has cleared the tower."

Many of us had never seen a live Space Shuttle launch. After 24 successful missions, launches weren't breaking new stories anymore; they were 20-second stories on the evening news. Other than liftoff, my classmates and I didn't know what to expect. When plumes of smoke erupted and snaked through the sky, we reacted with the same kind of surprise as when fireworks filled the sky. Some of my classmates stood up to get a closer view of the TV. When I stood up, I saw tears streaming down my teacher's face and knew something was horribly wrong.

I'm grateful that our teachers allowed us to continue watching the coverage after the explosion. We talked about sacrifice and loss. The teachers told us about previous tragedies in the space program in our quest to land a man on the moon. One teacher recounted for us the words from President John F. Kennedy's 1962 speech when he declared that the nation would go to the moon not because it was easy, but because it was hard. Five years of successful Space Shuttle launches made space exploration look easy for a whole new generation, when in reality, it was still very hard.

The Space Shuttle Challenger was the topic at my family's dinner table that night and for many nights and weeks to come. My father was an engineer, the serious kind who wore a pocket protector in his shirt pocket. It always contained a pen, a mechanical pencil, and a 6-inch mechanical ruler. I knew very little about the technical aspects of his job. He worked in the plastics industry, and I had one of every toy prototype his company made.

I was a daddy's girl. Many nights my father and I talked long after the evening news was over and long after my mother had lost interest in the conversation and cleared the table. I remember the tone and strength of my father's voice as he explained to me that the explosion was preventable. That evening, he got up from the dinner table, went out to the garage, and brought in an O-ring to show me what one looked like. It was a similar O-ring, though much larger, that failed on one of the Space Shuttle's solid rocket boosters that cold January in 1986. The rubber material of the O-ring became too stiff in the cold weather and failed to fully seal a critical joint, leading to an explosion that caused the loss of the Shuttle. My father patiently answered every question I had, either with an explanation, a sketch, or a piece of hardware in the garage.

It was in those weeks following the loss of the Space Shuttle Challenger that I developed a passion for aerospace. However, I never once considered being an astronaut. It was a risky job. I had just seen seven astronauts lose their lives in an explosion. Those conversations with my father created a desire within me to make a difference, but if I wasn't going to be an astronaut, how could I possibly make an impact?

I looked to my father for inspiration. I'd follow in his footsteps. He fixed things all the time at work. To hear him talk, some days that's all he did. His team relied on him to do things right the first time and work with everyone from the manufacturing floor to customer sites to solve problems. So, at age 11, I decided to become an aerospace engineer. With my father as my first mentor, I'd become the kind of person who found and fixed problems, the kind who made it safe for astronauts to fly.

Once I discovered my path, I never strayed in pursuit of that dream. I excelled in high school and was accepted into one of the top-rated aerospace engineering programs in the U.S. It was in the university setting that my dedication was first tested and my responses to challenges were shaped. There were tears and doubts and all-nighters and fears of not being good enough. I barely passed freshman Physics, a class fundamental to the field in which I dreamed of working. I went from being a perfectionist to getting my first 'D.' I was devastated. My GPA would be ruined, and I felt like it was finally exposed that I wasn't cut out to be an aerospace engineer. I couldn't admit it to my friends. I met with the professor, who matter-of-factly explained that it was a weed-out class. It was intended to make me reconsider my choice of majors and my career path. He went on to explain that I could retake the class or "move on." Move on?! That interpretation was left up to me, but I knew what he meant—move on with my 'D' or move on from aerospace engineering.

That conversation with someone who didn't understand my passion or my dream made me even more determined to succeed. I took the Physics course again the next semester and improved my grade with the help of a tutor. As my math courses got harder, sometimes a 'C' was the best I could muster. I'd review exams and homework to see where I went wrong and constantly learned from my mistakes. When friends dropped out of school and classmates changed majors, I became laser-focused on achieving my dream. I used that same focus and determination to get me through the rest of my classes, which never got any easier.

I soon found out that becoming an aerospace engineer was the easy part of my dream—being an aerospace engineer was the tough part.

After I entered the workforce, I quickly learned that how much

I knew and how well I did my job had little to do with my over-all success and ultimately, with the impact I could make. What mattered more was my reputation as a young woman, fresh out of college, who worked hard. Some colleagues stopped listening after the word "young." Being young isn't automatically associated with being knowledgeable and rarely is associated with experience. Others stopped listening after the word "woman." Few ever reached the words at the end of that sentence. Women are underrepresented in STEM fields in the United States. I'd entered a male-dominated field expecting to be outnumbered, but I didn't realize that my gender could be a disadvantage. I underestimated the effort required to both protect and improve my credibility every single day. Once I established my credibility, I had to earn the trust and respect of my peers. I perceived that my success reflected upon all female engineers, just as my mistakes would be projected onto female engineers as a whole.

Working in a climate where women have historically been excluded often makes me feel like I'm an imposter, even after so many years in the industry. As a young, female engineer, my confidence was tested daily. Imposter syndrome is more than just feeling like you don't belong. In my case, it was specifically tied to my expertise. I was afraid my colleagues would discover that I was unqualified for my job and didn't deserve my accomplishments. I wouldn't apply for a job unless I met 100% of the criteria in the job posting. In a far more career-limiting move, I wouldn't speak up in meetings for fear of asking a dumb question.

Where was the confidence I had when I wouldn't let my college physics professor impede my path to becoming an aerospace engineer? It turns out confidence didn't get me through college, perseverance did. I had those thoughts of being a fraud *and still performed well.* Several years into my career, I learned that what perseverance builds up, a lack of confidence will tear down. My doubts were limiting me from reaching my potential. How could I advance while struggling to feel that I deserved success? I looked inward. I looked for the opportunity. Just like my dad had taught me, I could be the kind of person who discovered underlying causal relationships, and before an explosion, I could remedy it, make it safe and have a lasting impact. And that's what I did.

First, I started to share what I'd learned. Sharing forced me to speak up, which was instrumental in building my credibility. With coaching from trusted mentors and role models, I started a women's network at my workplace to give other women a resource for mentoring, career development and support. I continue to strive to change the culture of my company from the inside out by investing in women and empowering them to cultivate their leadership skills, business acumen, and their networks. In making ourselves more visible and more vocal, our male allies started showing up for us. First, they showed up at our events, then they shared their knowledge as keynote speakers, then they became mentors and advisors. The number of women being promoted started to increase. I became a champion of diversity and inclusion in the workplace and developed a passion for mentoring. I became a catalyst for change and an expert in how to navigate in your career development when you're in the minority.

Second, I started to use what I'd learned. I'd become the kind of engineer who found and fixed problems. I realized I could improve processes to prevent problems and streamline processes to save time and money without sacrificing quality. I studied Lean Six Sigma (a certification program of principles and tools to reduce waste and improve process performance), earning a Green Belt, then a Black Belt. I am making a far bigger impact in my industry than I could have ever dreamed of in my childhood.

Focus, determination, and grit only got me so far in the early years of my career. Learning to appreciate and cultivate a support system was one of the biggest keys to my success. Mentors and coaches have been invaluable throughout my career. I have formal and informal mentoring relationships, technical mentors, and career coaches. The guidance of a trusted advisor can illuminate opportunities you never thought possible, and the trademark of a great coach is someone who challenges you to dream *bigger*.

While my confidence didn't grow overnight, stepping-stones appeared. Incremental change accelerated my career. I learned from every failure and there were many. I learned from each person willing to give me feedback, no matter how hard it was to hear at the time. Great mentoring helped me grow. Then, by exceeding expectations and building my reputation, I earned promotions. My credibility increased. Gaining the respect of my peers and leaders, including those who were much more experienced than I was, gave me the confidence to persevere into a new space.

I've learned that incremental process improvement can be applied to anything in your life. The simple act of identifying what is working and what isn't working can fuel your personal growth and your career growth at the same time. In fact, the reason that I know I'm still on track is that every time I face what seems like an impossible obstacle, I use my strategies and systems to break things down and build them back up into my new path forward.

Today, I have over 30 years' experience in staying true to my dream, even when it was hard. I have more than 20 years of experience in aerospace engineering. I've learned to navigate and even thrive in an environment where I didn't always fit. I'm now a leader in my industry, specifically chosen for my position because of the unique perspective and energy I bring to my role.

Over time, I changed the status quo by showing up, being seen and making my voice heard. That original inspired action I took after the Space Shuttle Challenger tragedy led to a successful career as an aerospace engineer, a process improvement expert, and now a respected leader. I'm not just an engineer—I fix things. I don't just improve things—I set new standards for excellence. Confidently acknowledging the capabilities and influence I have has made me realize that I can make an increasingly larger impact every time I give myself permission to dream bigger.

Comfortable. Courageous. Confident. I have stepped into my power. Rather than cringe, I smile with pride. I breathe gratitude, knowing I've earned my seat. I give myself permission to take up space, have you?

JENNIFER WRIGHT

Jennifer Wright has more than two decades of aerospace engineering, project management and technical leadership experience. She is a Lean Six-Sigma Black Belt because it's not enough for her to engineer things—she wants to improve them. Jennifer excels in streamlining technical processes and saves her company hundreds of labor hours and millions of dollars each year, earning her awards in Technical Excellence, Team Excellence, and International Business Development.

Jennifer is a champion of diversity and inclusion in the workplace. Her efforts were recognized with a corporate Diversity Award in 2011, received for founding a Women's Network to promote mentoring and professional development opportunities across her workplace.

Jennifer is passionate about STEM outreach, specifically being a role model for girls and young women who may not otherwise know that a technical career is attainable.

Jennifer is the proud mom of a young girl who wants to be the first veterinarian on Mars.

Learn more about partnering with Jennifer at www.jenniferwright.com.

PERMISSION TO CREATE
AN EXTRAORDINARY LIFE

JACQUE BOOK

The most important job I have ever done is raising my two children. They are the loves of my life, and at the end of my life, I know mothering them will be the thing I am most proud of.

For twenty-five years, I was a stay at home mom! I loved my job. I loved hearing the stories of what happened in their day as I was driving carpool after school. I loved making chocolate chip cookies for all their friends. I loved making a difference in their lives on the many occasions that I volunteered in their classes and chaperoned field trips.

One of my favorite memories was being a chaperone at a sleep away camp my daughter attended in sixth grade. We went to an outdoor camp on Catalina Island off the coast of southern California. Thank goodness we were sleeping in cabins, as I'm not really a sleeping bag kind of girl.

The boat ride to the island was amazing. It was a gorgeous sunny day, and we had the pleasure of watching hundreds of dolphins swim alongside the boat. When we landed on the island, we were given our cabin assignments. I was surprised that I had nine girls in my cabin, and I noticed that the other parent chaperones had three to four children in their cabins. I asked the teacher about it. She looked back at me, and said quietly, "Because we know you can handle it, and we're not so sure others can."

On the third night, a couple of Dads asked if the girls and I wanted to join them on top of the mountain to watch the sunrise. I have to admit I wasn't a huge fan of hiking or getting up when it was still dark, but I felt like it would be a great experience for all of us. So, I had a meeting with the girls because the catch was everyone goes or no one goes. I went to bed that night hoping all the girls would be up for the adventure.

In the morning, everyone was up and dressed, flashlights in hand, and ready to go. As we progressed up the mountain, I realized this was not a stroll—it was straight up. At one point, I was not sure I was going to make it. My fear of heights kicked in. As I turned a corner and looked up, one of the dads reached out his arm to grab mine. It all happened so fast. I think he literally pulled me up that part of the hike. We all made it up to the top of the mountain in plenty of time for sunrise. This is one of my favorite stories because it was not common for me to agree to do things out of my comfort zone, but this time, I did; and I had an unbelievable experience. What I learned that day is that it is invaluable to try new things, step out of my comfort zone, and walk through my fears.

Sitting on top of that mountain, I realized I hadn't worked outside the home in many years. I thought, when the kids were all grown, *what would I do next? What talents did I have? Who would hire me?* These doubts sent me into a downward spiral. Do you ever have these thoughts? You might be looking at a mountain that you think is too big to climb but know that everyone's mountain is different. There are people along the way that will pull you up like they did me.

As I think about it in retrospect, a stay at home mom has so many skills that could help her land her dream job. She's a chauffeur, chef, event planner, time-manager, house cleaner, not to mention a chief negotiator. She has great communications skills, organizational skills, research skills, and she often has eyes in the back of her head!

Second Act!

A pivotal moment in my life took place on Super Bowl Sunday, 2016. I ran into a friend that I hadn't seen in a while. I told her I was looking for a job as a personal assistant. I needed to shift into the next chapter of my life since my job as a stay at home mom had been terminated. Both my children had moved out of the house to pursue their college educations.

My friend, Patty, got a funny look on her face and said, "My company thinks that I need an assistant!"

A few weeks later, Patty called and said, "I want you to come to work for me! When can you start?"

I was on my way to get a few things at Costco and told her I could come over when I finished.

She said, "Great, I will text you a list of what I need at Costco!"

In that moment, I gave myself permission to re-create my life, as I knew it. I would step out of my comfort zone of being a stay at home mom and housewife and begin to create a new career.

In the beginning of my new career with Jack Canfield and Patty Aubery, my days were full of new experiences. As with any new job, there is a learning curve. You must get to know who people are; what the company does; what the priorities are; and how to smoothly orchestrate all the details. I began by cleaning up thousands of emails, unsubscribing from the non-essential ones, and learning how to properly answer the important ones. Next, I learned all of the products and trainings offered by the company.

Then it was time to get to know those products and trainings for myself because you can know all the ingredients in a chocolate cake, but until you eat one, you don't know how it tastes. I attended a weeklong training called BTS. It was a life-changing week for me. Jack Canfield was on stage from morning till night, teaching us valuable Success Principles, leading meditations, facilitating small group exercises where we shared deeply personal things with complete strangers. I learned three crucial things at this training to bring into my daily life.

Event+Response=Outcome!

In every situation in our life, we have control of one thing, our RESPONSE. We can't change the Event, but we could change the Outcome. I learned if I don't like the outcomes I was experiencing, I needed to change the way I was responding to the Event! That was huge; my responses were where my power was.

Affirmations!

It is crucial for success to create and say Affirmations daily! One of my favorite ones to say is, "I am so grateful and thankful that money flows into and out of my home from expected and unexpected places!"

Visualizations!

I learned that you have to know exactly what you want. The universe is happy to give you everything you want, but it is not a mind reader. I got busy creating a vision board. I put everything I wanted to create and manifest in my life on it. I visualized myself experiencing a fantastic vacation in Italy: what it looked like, what it smelled like, the salty water, the glorious meal being prepared for me, who I was with, what I was seeing from my villa. I was creating my ideal vision, allowing me to attract it into my life. I believe we can believe anything into being, even our biggest scariest dreams. In 2018 I spent a glorious two weeks in Tuscany with my husband who happens to be the love of my life! I envisioned this trip years before it happened!

Working with Jack Canfield, I had the opportunity to learn mindset strategies and success principles from one of the best teachers in the world! As a bonus, I became a certified trainer. Through the years, I was able make deep connections with new friends across the globe, inspire many people, and have more travel adventures than I could have ever dreamed possible. Every moment of every day, I choose to live a grateful and purposeful life. I hope that you too choose this for your life! I gave myself permission to live my dream life. The life I was put on this earth to be, to do, and to have.

One of the things I am grateful for is to have Patty Aubery as my mentor. She believed in me, gave me a lot of responsibility, space to learn, and new things to tackle. When I made mistakes along the way, which I did, she was always there to guide me. Everyone needs a little inspiration and support from others who see the greatness in them. When I released my fear of believing I was not qualified to work outside the home, I gained the confidence to believe in myself and say yes to magnificent new opportunities. Through this I have learned that my mission is to empower, support, and inspire women to live their dream life.

We all have the power to re-create our life from status quo to extraordinary. I have been researching energy and healing for twenty-five years, and I learned that I have a superpower. I am a light healer and an inspirational tuning fork. I hope this encourages you to use your superpowers, believe that anything is possible, and have the confidence to make it happen. It's time to step out of your comfort zone and as scary as it feels, begin to dream bigger than you ever have before! We each have unique talents. Magic happens when we own our powerful unique qualities and play full out in this one beautiful life because that is where the miracles begin to happen!

JACQUE BOOK

Jacque Book is a mindset strategist and an inspirational speaker. As a certified success coach, Jacque's passion is to educate women in all walks of life, including business owners and moms, to cultivate heart and soul connections to feel empowered. She uses strategies on mindfulness, positive self-talk, meditation, heart connections, and energy shifting techniques with her clients giving them the tools and permission to live an extraordinary life.

Shortly after transitioning from being a full-time mom, she was diagnosed with broken heart syndrome, which left part of her heart tissue medically dead. Using her own techniques, she was able to fully heal her heart. More on that story in her upcoming book.

Besides her love of being a mom and wife, she also has a passion for creating healing jewelry. Her custom brand is called Jacque Christine Designs. She is an Ambassador for GoalFriends, and a #1 bestselling author in Oola for Women. Jacque says if she can live an extraordinary life so can you.

You can connect with Jacque, by visiting her website www.JacqueBook.com, where you can find her programs, books, inspirational products and receive a Free "Light Healing Meditation".

Instagram: @jacquebook @jacquechristinedesigns
Facebook: @jacquebookcoaching @jacquechristinedesigns

*Permission is Granted
to live out your
wildest dreams.*

Your time is now.

the Permission Granted authors

REPRINTED WITH PERMISSIONS

Iyanla Vanzant

Patty Aubery

Kate Butler

Bronwen Talley-Coffey

Samantha Ruth

Lindsay Smith

Marci Shimoff

Amy Shonka

Juli Facer Scarbrough

Cheryl Howell

Lisa Nichols

Jewell Siebert

Maggie Sullivan

Donna Nudel Brown

Jennifer Granger

Janet Attwood

Tonya Lisenby Hendley

Lori Creech Phillips

Darlene Whitehurst

Jennifer Wright

Jacque Book

DO YOU HAVE A STORY YOU'D LIKE TO SHARE?
Send it in to Kate and Patty at kate&patty@pattyaubery.com

www.ingramcontent.com/pod-product-compliance
Lightning Source LLC
Chambersburg PA
CBHW071158130626
46553CB00004B/1711

* 9 7 9 8 9 8 8 3 1 8 4 1 5 *